HISTORIC ALEXANDRIA

An Illustrated History

Second Edition, Abridged

by Ted Pulliam

Published by HPNbooks, a Division of Ledge Media

Second Edition, Abridged

Copyright © 2024 HPNbooks

All rights reserved. No part of this book may be reproduced in any form or by any means, electronic or mechanical, including photocopying, without permission in writing from the publisher. All inquiries should be addressed to Ledge Media, P.O. Box 230054, Encinitas CA 92023. Phone (833) 533-4363, www.hpnbooks.com.

ISBN: 979-8-89177-067-6

Library of Congress Card Catalog Number: 2024947035

Historic Alexandria: An Illustrated History

author:	Ted Pulliam
cover artist:	John M. Barber

HPNbooks/Ledge Media

publisher & CEO:	Daphne Fletcher
VP & Director of IT:	Rafael Ramirez
administration:	Kevin Hearn
production:	Colin Hart
	Christopher D. Sturdevant

CONTENTS

ACKNOWLEDGMENTS

I am indebted to many people for helping to pull this book together: My special thanks to Rita Holtz for her extremely skillful work finding, obtaining, and assembling the photographs, drawings, and other images for the book. Thanks also to Diane Riker and Bob Madison for reading early versions of the text and for their incisive comments and to Bob for encouraging me to write the book. I also am grateful to: Wally Owen, Jim Johnston, George Combs, Bunny Jacob, Jim Mackay, and Pam Cressey for reading parts of the text and their very helpful suggestions; Pam Cressey, Steve Shephard, Fran Bromberg, Barbara Magid, and Ruth Reeder of Alexandria Archaeology for their help and encouragement; George Combs, Leslie Morales, Mark Zoeter, and Julie Downie of the Local History/Special Collections Branch of the Alexandria Library for their very capable help with research and images; Marilyn Whiteman, Chrystal Willet, and Frimble Smith for their research on particular subjects; Jackie Cohan in the Alexandria Archives and Records Center; Lance Malamo and Amy Bertsch of the Office of Historic Alexandria; and T. Michael Miller and all the men and women who have written on the history of Alexandria before me. Most of all, my thanks to Molly for whom I have the greatest love.

Ted Pulliam
September 2010

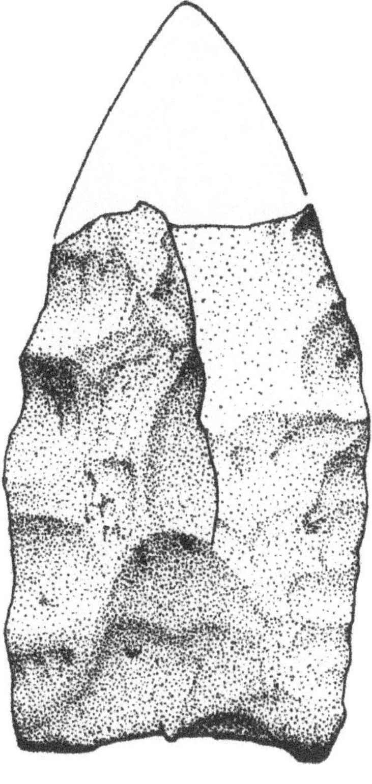

CHAPTER I

THE FIRST PEOPLES

In August 2007, archaeologists working for the City of Alexandria were digging at the site of the Contrabands and Freedmen's Cemetery at the intersection of Church and South Washington Streets. Although their main task was to locate graves of the more than eighteen hundred runaway slaves and free African Americans buried there during and immediately after the Civil War, they soon found signs that part of the site was used much earlier.

An archaeologist searching where such signs were found used a trowel to scrape dirt from a designated square and place it into a bucket. Later someone sifted through the dirt for artifacts, found several stone points (mainly spear points), and put them aside. One had its tip broken off.

Only later, when Fairfax County Senior Archaeologist Mike Johnson examined the points, was it discovered by its shape and workmanship that the broken one was the oldest yet found in Alexandria, a Clovis Point estimated to be thirteen thousand years old, the earliest sign of human presence in the Alexandria area.

In that extremely remote time, the Indian who made the point would have been one of a small band of hunter-foragers moving through the Alexandria area grasslands (there were as yet no forests there) searching for food. The Indian must have sat down, and while forming a bit of quartzite into a point, broke off its tip. The point now was ruined. He discarded it, got up, and moved on.

This Indian was a predecessor of the Algonquians who lived in the Alexandria area when the first Englishmen appeared and a predecessor of the Europeans, Africans, and people from many parts of the world who eventually came to live in Alexandria.

❖

The photograph on the left shows the spear point (actual size approximately 1 1/4 inches long, 3/4 inches wide, and 1/4 inch thick). The drawing on the right shows how the point would have looked if whole.

PHOTO COURTESY OF ALEXANDRIA ARCHAEOLOGY.
DRAWING BY ANDREW H. FLORA.

Today it is little noticed that the City of Alexandria is bordered on three sides by water —on the east by the Potomac River, on the south by Great Hunting Creek and Cameron Run, and on the north by Four Mile Run. However, this characteristic would not have gone unnoticed by the Algonquians who had established homes in the Alexandria area by the late 1500s. In fact, to them this border would have been the most important geographical fact of the Alexandria area.

The Algonquians sought home sites that offered several advantages. They wanted fresh-water marshes where women could gather plants—reeds for making houses and tuckahoe for food—and shallow fresh-water creeks where men would catch spawning fish. They liked level ground along a river for planting crops. Home sites with forests nearby were valued for deer, nuts, and firewood. The Algonquians also sought rounded stones from creek bottoms that they could use to form a variety of tools, including arrowheads and spear points.

Once Algonquians found a suitable site, they would raise houses by inserting into the ground the ends of several flexible young trees, bending them over, and tying the other ends together in the form of an upside down

bowl or stubby rectangle. Then they would cover these forms with layers of bark or with mats made from reeds sewn together. A hole would be left in the roof for smoke from an interior fire to exit, and an opening left in a side for a door that could be covered with reed mats for warmth. Archaeological traces of such a house site dating back to a pre-Algonquian era have been found on Jones Point in Alexandria. It probably was used during the spring and summer fishing season.

In July 1608 the Alexandria area Algonquians would have seen a strange water craft coming up the Potomac River. It was a small, open boat propelled by a sail and oars, called a barge or shallop, and on board were 28-year-old Captain John Smith and 14 Englishmen from Jamestown, the first Europeans to come to the Alexandria area.

They did not land here but proceeded on up the river to the falls just above present-day Georgetown. There they disembarked and walked the banks of the river searching in vain for the "glistering metal," gold.

In proceeding back down river, Smith noted on a carefully-prepared map the Algonquian village of Assaomeck ("middle fishing place") at what appears to be just south of Great Hunting Creek. As its name suggests,

❖

Above: Some different Algonquian fishing techniques: wooden fish trap, spear fishing, and fishing with poles, plus a canoe filled with big fish and a fire to cook them.
COURTESY OF JOHN CARTER BROWN LIBRARY, BROWN UNIVERSITY. DRAWING BY JOHN WHITE.

Below: This portrait of Captain John Smith appeared in the corner of a map in Smith's Description of New England published in 1616 when Smith was thirty-six years old, eight years after he passed by the future Alexandria on a boat trip on the Potomac River..
COURTESY OF WIKIMEDIA COMMONS. ENGRAVING BY SIMON VAN DE PASSE.

Smith did find one commodity on the Potomac that would benefit future European occupants of Alexandria. The river teemed with fish. As he recorded "in divers places that aboundance of fish, lying so thicke with their heads above the water, as for want of nets (our barge driving amongst them) we attempted to catch them with a frying pan, but we found it a bad instrument to catch fish with."

For a number of years after Smith's visit, there were few other European visitors to the upper Potomac other than a handful of traders who came by ship to trade for the Indians' corn and furs.

Then in the late 1640s a wealthy refugee from religious and personal conflicts in Maryland, Giles Brent, crossed the river with his teenaged Piscataway Indian wife and established his home at Aquia Creek, about 35 miles south of the future Alexandria, and became the northernmost European on the Virginia side of the Potomac. Soon joining him was his formidable sister Margaret. In Maryland Margaret Brent had been a close associate of Governor Leonard Calvert and had appeared so often in the local courts handling business matters, which was particularly unusual for a woman, that she was listed in some court records as "Mistress Margaret Brent, Gentleman."

Around the time of the Brents' arrival, there was a land rush along the Potomac. A treaty Virginia signed in 1646 with the remnants of Powhatan Indians, Algonquians who had long controlled a vast area of the colony, prohibited colonists from traveling north of the York River, but Virginia unilaterally nullified it effective September 1649, opening the Potomac River for settlement. The historian Robert Moxham estimated that between 1651 and 1679, "nearly a hundred colonial patents [land grants] were given, conveying rights to many thousands of acres of the Potomac waterfront from the Occoquan River to Great Falls."

One of those many patents went in 1654 to Margaret Brent, then in her early 50s, for 700 acres on Great Hunting Creek. Hers included much of present-day Old Town Alexandria and was the town's first land grant.

Fifteen years later, in April 1669, a landowner from Stafford County named John Alexander sailed upriver to survey land just south of Great Hunting Creek for John Washington (George Washington's great-grandfather), land that later became Mount Vernon. After completing his survey, he probably directed his boat a little further upriver past the future Alexandria site and around the bend to see what was there.

Apparently he liked what he saw but lacked sufficient headrights, credits given at the rate of fifty acres for each person transported to Virginia, that were necessary then to acquire land in the colony. However, a neighboring tobacco merchant, Robert Howson, did have the needed headrights.

On October 21, 1669, Howson used his headrights to patent the land from the Governor of Virginia, and within a month, John Alexander purchased it from him for 6,000 pounds of tobacco. John Alexander's new purchase included not only the future site of Alexandria, but also what would become Reagan Washington National Airport, the Pentagon, and Arlington National Cemetery.

It also included the seven hundred acres Margaret Brent had purchased earlier, although for a while no one noticed. After her death, however, her heirs discovered John Alexander's purchase and in 1675 forced Alexander to pay them 10,500 pounds of tobacco for their interest in the property, more than he earlier had paid Howson for his whole grant. Finally,

❖

Farmers of small holdings who first lived at the site of the future Alexandria in the late 1600s may have lived in houses that resembled this one painted by Sidney King for the 350th anniversary of the founding of Jamestown.

however, John Alexander owned the Alexandria area and much more.

By this time, many of the Algonquians who had lived so long in the Alexandria area were there no longer. Diseases they contracted from contact with European traders and settlers and to which they had no immunity took a significant toll. Also a factor in their disappearance were attacks by the Iroquoian-speaking Susquehannoks, fierce warriors whom Captain John Smith thought in 1608 to be much more impressive than the Algonquians ("Such great and well proportioned men are seldom seene, for they seemed like Giants to the English, yea and to the neighbors").

The first clear indication that there was a European living in the area that is now Alexandria was when John Alexander wrote his will on October 25, 1677. He left 200 acres to Elizabeth Holmes (as well as a bed, but not "the best bed") and described the 200 acres as being on land "where John Coggins lives." Later deeds and maps locate the 200 acres in an area in present-day Alexandria bounded on the east by Hooff's Run, the north by Duke Street, the south by the old channel of Great Hunting Creek/Cameron Run, and the west about half way to Telegraph Road. (In another hundred years, this area would be called "West End" and now is called "Carlyle.") There Coggins had a house, possibly made of logs, that stood near a spring.

Nothing is known about Coggins other than his name. He probably was a tenant or employee of John Alexander. However, he did not stay there permanently but was driven away in the early 1680s by incursions and alarms of hostile Indians, mainly Susquehannoks from Pennsylvania and Maryland and the fierce Iroquois from upstate New York.

Settlers did not return to the area until the late 1680s. In 1686, Robert Alexander, a descendant of John Alexander, conveyed to Ralph Platt land on a channel (shown on early maps as "Ralph's Gut") that flowed through a marsh and into what is now Oronoco Bay. About the same time, on other Alexander land Robert Alexander established quarters that probably consisted of a few buildings, slaves, and an overseer.

Gradually, other settlers joined them. In some cases, the new households were headed by women—Judith Ballenger and Sarah Amos rented land from Robert Alexander below Four Mile Run in the early 1730s.

How did these early settlers survive? Once they had cleared fields, some with the help of slaves, they focused on the time-consuming process of growing tobacco, the crop that made them the most money. In fact, tobacco was used as money through notes from one planter to another giving the possessor of the note the right to a certain quantity of tobacco. Like money, such notes passed from hand to hand to pay debts. Settlers also raised cattle and hogs and let them run "wilde in the woods" that grew between their widely scattered homes.

T O B A C C O   I N S P E C T I O N
S T A T I O N

In 1730 there were enough settlers in the area that when the Virginia General Assembly established a system of tobacco inspection stations throughout the colony that year, it established an inspection station "upon Broadwater's land" on the south bank of Great Hunting Creek near its mouth. Two years later, however, the General Assembly found this site to be "very inconvenient," and it established a new inspection station at the point of land that once belonged to Ralph

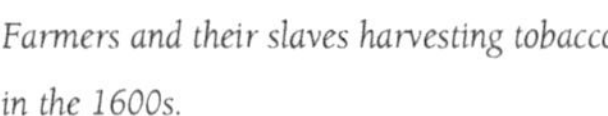

❖

Farmers and their slaves harvesting tobacco in the 1600s.

COURTESY OF JAMESTOWN-YORKTOWN EDUCATIONAL TRUST. PAINTING BY SIDNEY KING.

Platt but was then owned by Simon Pearson, who already had built a warehouse there.

This point, located at the foot of present-day Oronoco Street, was the northern point of a shallow bay that to the south curved inward and back out again to another point at the foot of present-day Duke Street. Although this new site was located about a mile from the first warehouse site, it still was known as Hunting Creek Warehouse.

Sometime between 1735 and 1739, Pearson deeded this land and the warehouse to Hugh West, from Stafford County. Hugh West took over the public warehouse and expanded his holdings on the point to include a ferry to Maryland and an ordinary (tavern). The point soon became known as West or West's Point.

About the same time, a small community called Cameron began to develop at the head of Great Hunting Creek (roughly where now Telegraph Road crosses the beltway) where the main north-south roads crossed the creek and met a road heading west. Great Hunting Creek was then navigable by ships at high tide some way up toward its head, giving the community commercial connections by both ground and water. Soon it could boast of an ordinary and a few houses, and soon also it would rival West's Point as the possible site for a new town.

SEEKING A NEW TOWN

In the 1740s, Fredericksburg was the northern-most town on the Virginia side of the Potomac River. However, the powerful Fairfax family, young Scottish factors (business agents), and influential planters living in the northern part of Virginia thought this situation should change. They realized that western Virginia was opening up for settlers, and these newcomers needed a port on the upper Potomac where they could sell their crops and buy the goods they needed and desired.

Thus the Journal for the House of Burgesses reported that on November 1, 1748, "Inhabitants of Fairfax [County]" petitioned the General Assembly (composed of an elected House of Burgesses and an appointed Governor's Council acting in its legislative

capacity) to establish a town "at Hunting-Creek Warehouse, on Patowmack River," that is, at West's Point.

The petition has not survived, but it probably specified that the new town be built on land owned by Hugh West, John Alexander, and Philip Alexander. The petition's signers very likely included Thomas, Lord Fairfax, owner of the vast amount of land between the Rappahannock and Potomac Rivers all the way from the Chesapeake Bay to the rivers' headwaters, and his relations: his cousin and land agent William Fairfax; William Fairfax's son-in-law Lawrence Washington, a burgess from Fairfax County; and John Carlyle, an energetic merchant and William Fairfax's son-in-law to be.

The Fairfax petition was supported by a petition from the "Inhabitants of Frederick County" (Winchester). Lord Fairfax owned much of the land in Frederick County and likely was behind this petition also, along with a burgess from Frederick County, William Fairfax's son, George William Fairfax.

Around the same time Lawrence Washington's sixteen year old half-brother George drew a map of the land around the crescent bay on which the new town was to be built. He inscribed on the map the type of

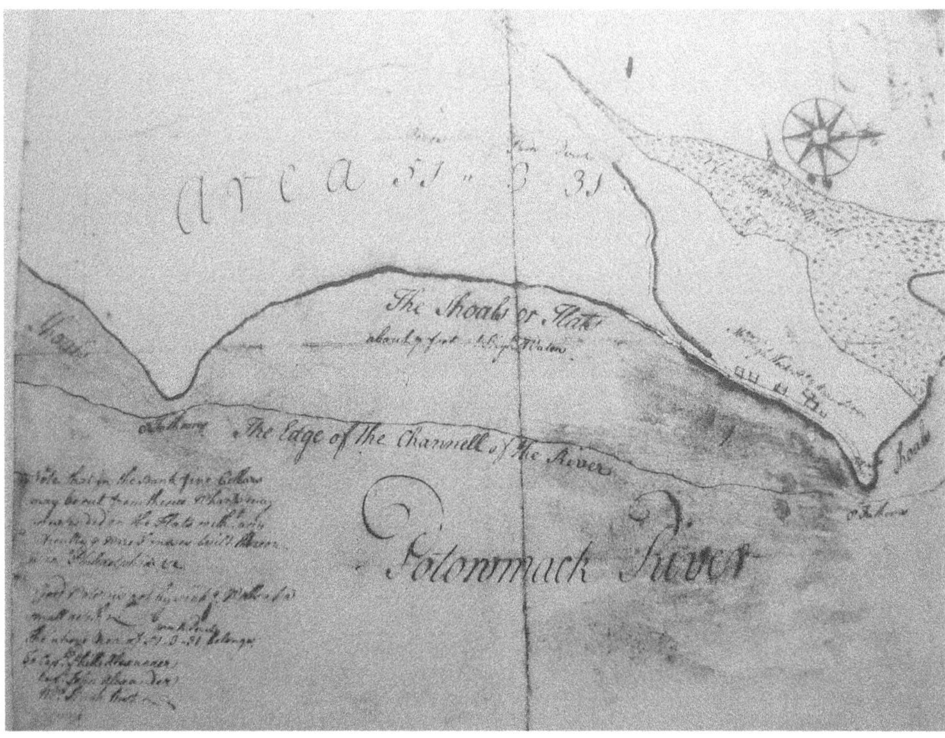

❖

George Washington's map of the future site of Alexandria in 1748 showing the crescent-shaped bay and the Hunting Creek Warehouse complex on the point to the right. Unlike modern maps, which are oriented so that north is at the top, this map places west at the top. At that time, much travel was by boat or ship, thus maps frequently were oriented to be viewed as if approaching from water, in this case the Potomac River.

COURTESY OF THE LIBRARY OF CONGRESS.

lines a modern real estate agent would applaud: "Note that in the Bank fine Cellars may be cut from thence wharfs may be extended on the Flats without any difficulty & Ware Houses built thereon as in Philadelphia."

As the petitioners learned, however, one of the owners of the land where the town was to be built, Philip Alexander, had no desire to sell his property. He immediately submitted to the House of Burgesses a petition that opposed the West's Point location and favored instead locating the town at Cameron, the small community at the head of Great Hunting Creek.

The three petitions, the ones from Fairfax and Frederick counties and the one from Philip Alexander, were referred to a House committee. When the committee finally reported to the House on April 5, 1749, it recommended rejecting all three. Philip Alexander appeared to have won.

The Fairfax family's influence, however, ultimately proved too strong. Burgess Lawrence Washington probably led the fight for the Fairfax County petition in the House of Burgesses, which rejected the committee's recommendation and instead ordered a bill to be prepared creating a town at Hunting Creek

Warehouse. On April 22 the bill passed the House and, two days later, Lawrence Washington presented the bill to the Governor's Council. After inserting a few amendments, the Council agreed to the bill, which undoubtedly had Council member William Fairfax's strong support. The House later agreed to the amended bill, and May 11, 1749, the Governor signed the bill into law.

The West's Point supporters had a new town where they wanted it. Possibly as a sop to Philip Alexander, it was called Alexandria.

Appointed by the Assembly as the new town's first trustees and founders were: the influential nobleman landowner, Thomas Lord Fairfax; Governor's Council member William Fairfax; his son Burgess George William Fairfax; Lawrence Washington and Richard Osborn, the two burgesses from Fairfax County; John Carlyle, factor for an English shipping firm; Hugh West, proprietor of the Hunting Creek warehouse and West's Point; John Pagan and William Ramsay, young Scottish factors; Gerrard Alexander, brother of John Alexander, one of the town's landowners; and lastly, Philip Alexander. All but the last had supported the bill. They now set out to build a town.

Chapter II
A New Town, 1749-1764

THE FIRST AUCTION

On July 13, 1749, a crowd composed mainly of men gathered at the site of the future Alexandria for an auction of the new town's eighty-four lots.

The site was some 60 acres of worn out tobacco fields bordered on the east primarily by 15- to 20-foot bluffs that dropped sharply down to the shores of a shallow bay of the Potomac River. The bay itself curved gradually inward from its southern point (Point Lumley) and then curved gradually back out again to a northern point (called West's Point after its owner Hugh West). Only at West's Point did the land slope down from the bluffs to water level. On that point stood the official Hunting Creek tobacco warehouse, Hugh West's house, a ferry landing, a tavern, and a few other bare wooden buildings.

The site had been surveyed earlier by John West, Jr., Hugh West's son and deputy surveyor of Fairfax County. West also staked the lots and drew a map of the future town. (Young George Washington later copied West's map, probably for his half-brothers, Lawrence and Augustine.)

West's and Washington's maps showed the town lots and grid with seven streets running west, away from the Potomac, and three streets running north and south, parallel to the river. The street names honored royalty, nobility, and the influential Fairfax family, except for Water Street, the street closest to the river (now Lee Street), and Oronoco, named after a type of tobacco.

On that July day, auctioneer John West, Jr., struck off the first lot, lot 36, to John Dalton, a 26-year-old merchant originally from Gloucester County, Virginia. The lot was well located on the edge of the bluffs overlooking the river and on the north side of Cameron Street. Dalton later also bought adjoining lot 37 on the corner of Cameron and Fairfax Streets.

Another young merchant, 29-year-old John Carlyle from a Dumfrieshire family, bought two lots on the same side of Fairfax Street as Dalton and just across Cameron Street from him. Thirty-three- year-old

❖

General Braddock shown as he is shot in his battle with the French and Indians. George Washington is depicted grasping the bridle of Braddock's horse as Braddock falls mortally wounded.

COURTESY OF WISCONSIN HISTORICAL SOCIETY. PAINTING BY EDWIN WILLARD DEMING.

William Ramsay, originally from the Galloway district of Kircudbrightshire, bought lots adjoining John Carlyle, Fairfax Street, King Street, and the waterfront. These three men, who lived in a line along Fairfax Street, soon would become the new town's leaders.

Before the auction, these three, along with Lawrence Washington and Nathaniel Chapman, secretly bought the part of the new town site that belonged to Philip Alexander. Alexander had never wanted the town on his land and feared he would receive little for it at auction, so he made his deal with the five men earlier. Then at the auction, each of the five bought lots, and afterward they divided among themselves the profits from the sale of Alexander's land after discounting the price of the lots each purchased.

The auction lasted two days. The two points at each end of town, West's Point and Point Lumley, plus a market square on half the block bordered by King, Royal, Cameron, and Fairfax Streets purposely were not sold but were reserved for public use. Although not all the lots were sold then, the new town was off to a good start.

A TOWN GROWS

The trustees required a lot owner to build a house on his lot within two years of purchase or lose it (a requirement loosely enforced). Most lot owners met the requirement by erecting small, wooden structures on their lots. Around 1751, John Dalton built a clapboard house on his Fairfax Street lot. (It may still exist behind the facade of the house at 207 North Fairfax Street.) Soon after the auction, William Ramsay likely used boards and other material from older buildings to construct a new home at 221 King Street. (A 1956 reconstruction is now the Alexandria Visitors Center)

John Carlyle, however, built between Dalton's and Ramsay's a different home, a Palladian-style, two-story house with unusual sandstone outer walls that stood back on his lot on Fairfax Street. When he moved into it in August 1753, it was the grandest in town. (It still stands today).

Carlyle, a town trustee, a justice of the Fairfax County Court, and the son-in-law of the influential William Fairfax, was a man on the move. Possibly as early as 1753, he and Dalton went into business together, mainly exporting tobacco and selling goods from incoming ships' cargo. It would be a long-lasting and successful partnership. Similarly, Ramsay teamed up with John Dixon to export tobacco and sell imported goods.

Carlyle and the other town leaders began to use their influence. In February 1752 the Virginia General Assembly allowed Alexandria to have two fairs a year, in May and October, "for the sale and vending of all manner of cattle, victuals, provisions, goods, wares, and merchandizes." Only two months later, the Assembly ordered the Fairfax County courthouse and jail moved from near present-day Tysons Corner to Alexandria, where the Court met for the first time in May.

Market Square became the site of the county courthouse, jail, stocks, and pillory, and an open market where farmers sold horses, chickens, vegetables, meat, and fruit. It also may have been the place where in 1750 Dalton sold 25 slaves that he imported, probably from Barbados. If so, it was the first sale of slaves in Alexandria.

For spiritual matters, Alexandrians gathered every third Sunday to hear a parson preach an Anglican service at a chapel probably located at Pitt and Princess Streets.

In 1753, Britain's long-time enemy France began building a chain of forts south from Canada down the Allegheny River in order to block British colonists in Pennsylvania and Virginia from expanding westward into the Ohio Country. Robert Dinwiddie, acting governor of Virginia, responded by sending 21-year-old George Washington to the French to inform them that Virginia claimed the Ohio and to persuade them to halt. Young Washington, however, spoke no French and had no diplomatic experience. The French were unimpressed and continued building.

In January 1754 Washington reported the dismissive French response to Governor Dinwiddie. The affronted governor ordered Washington immediately to gather militia units at Alexandria and there to "train & discipline them in the best Manner You can" in preparation for a return to the Ohio to build British forts to block the French.

Governor Dinwiddie also commissioned John Carlyle as commissary in charge of providing Washington's forces with supplies ("a sufficient Quantity of Flower, Bread, Beef and Pork for 500 Men for six or eight months"). Carlyle made his headquarters in Alexandria.

Washington, however, had little time to drill his new troops on Alexandria's Market Square. The French were moving south faster than anticipated, and on March 15, Governor Dinwiddie ordered Washington to leave Alexandria for the Ohio Country as quickly as possible with "what Soldiers You have enlisted."

On April 2, Washington marched out of Alexandria with only about 120 soldiers, several officers, and "one Swedish Gentleman, who was a Volunteer." One of the officers was John West, Jr., the deputy surveyor of Fairfax County who laid out the Alexandria lots. Also accompanying Washington was Dr. James Craik, later an Alexandria resident and Washington's life-long friend, and a sergeant named Thomas Longdon, an ancestor of Samuel Snowden, later editor of the *Alexandria Gazette.*

On May 28, Washington, now in Pennsylvania and reinforced by a few additional soldiers, attacked and defeated a small party of Frenchmen. Although he did not know it, he had fired the first shots of the French and Indian War.

Soon after this initial success, Washington and his men were themselves attacked at a hastily erected fort at Great Meadows, which the inexperienced Washington called "a charming field for an Encounter." There they were soundly defeated and surrendered. On July 4, 1754, the French, not officially at war with Great Britain, allowed them to return to Virginia.

Meanwhile, Carlyle had trouble supplying Washington's soldiers. His trouble only increased after Washington and his men returned and Virginia began to recruit troops to fight the French again. Governor Dinwiddie wrote to Carlyle in June, August, September, and December 1754 to pass on from the Governor's Council and several officers, including Washington, complaints of his "not having discharged your duty...with the Exactness and Dispatch expected."

Carlyle realized he had taken on a huge task. He wrote to his family in England that it was "the most Troublesome one I ever had."

Then in January 1755, Carlyle received word that his task was to become even more troublesome—an entire British army under General Edward Braddock was coming to Alexandria.

GENERAL BRADDOCK'S
ARMY ARRIVES

In March 1755, the first of 17 ships loaded with British soldiers and their supplies and

❖

The William Ramsay House, 221 King Street, c. the 1920s.
COURTESY OF THE ALEXANDRIA LIBRARY, SPECIAL COLLECTIONS, MORRIS LOEB COLLECTION.

❖

Above: A sketch of John Carlyle's House, 121 North Fairfax Street, as it would have appeared when General Edward Braddock made it his headquarters.
COURTESY OF THE ALEXANDRIA LIBRARY, SPECIAL COLLECTIONS.

Below: "A Charming Field for an Encounter." George Washington's soldiers aligned in front of Fort Necessity at Great Meadows in western Pennsylvania before their defeat there by the French and Indians. The red uniforms look the same as those worn later by General Braddock's British troops, except that the wide lapels and turned-back cuffs of Braddock's men were different colors to denote their different regiments.
COURTESY OF PARAMOUNT PRESS, INC. PAINTING BY ROBERT GRIFFING.

weapons docked at the landing at West's Point at the foot of Oronoco Street. Immediately the 48th Regiment of Foot began to disembark and form into ranks.

They must have made a striking scene with each man wearing his long, bright red coat with its dull yellow lapels and wide, dull yellow cuffs and his bright red breeches whose legs were tucked into white leggings that buttoned over his knees, half-way up his thigh. On his head a private wore a flat, black tricorn hat edged in white, and a special grenadier wore his distinctive tall, narrow hat shaped like a tombstone with a thin metal plate in front.

Once they had formed up, they began to march up Oronoco and down Fairfax Streets. Townsmen, housewives, children, and servants stood in front of log or wood-frame houses to watch and cheer as the redcoats, their fifes squealing, drums beating, regimental flag flapping, passed up the dusty streets scattering hogs, geese, and dogs from their path.

Before arrival of the army, the town's population was a little over five hundred. The British soldiers tripled that number, and with the arrival of new recruits for the British and Virginia forces, the population increased further, vastly overcrowding the town's few available rooms. Mrs. Charlotte Brown, a nurse traveling with Braddock's army, wrote in her diary that she went to every house in Alexandria in search of lodging and "at last was Obliged to take a Room but little larger than to hold my Bed, and not so much as a Chair in it."

One of Braddock's soldiers walking Alexandria's streets was Lt. Col. Thomas Gage. Twenty years later, in April 1775, Gage would be royal governor of Massachusetts and send British troops to Lexington and Concord, causing Paul Revere to ride and the minutemen to rally and helping to precipitate the American Revolution.

General Braddock himself did not reach Alexandria until March 26, arriving with Governor Dinwiddie in the governor's handsome coach. The general quickly obtained for himself the best house in Alexandria, John Carlyle's stone mansion. It was here on April 14 that he assembled what John Carlyle labeled "the Grandest Congress…ever known on This Continent." The colonial governors of Massachusetts, New York, Pennsylvania, and Maryland, along with Dinwiddie of Virginia, met there with Braddock to discuss military and financial strategy.

The principal action they agreed on over the three-day conference was to attack the French at four points: Fort Duquesne at the confluence of the Monongahela and the Allegheny Rivers (the site of present-day Pittsburgh and Braddock's initial objective) and forts in New York (at Niagara and Crown Point) and in Nova Scotia.

Yet who would pay for these operations? Not the colonies, at least not voluntarily, the governors reported. Their legislatures would refuse to provide the funds. Instead, the ministers in London should find a way to compel them to do so. As a result, in his letter to London about the conference, Braddock reported that London must levy "a Tax" directly upon the colonies for the needed funds.

Some historians have wondered whether this report could have led to the British Stamp Act of 1765. As historian Lawrence Henry Gipson noted, however, a stamp tax for the colonies had been suggested as early as 1722, and suggested again in 1754, the year before the Alexandria conference. The Alexandria conference's recommendation may have added to the cumulative effect of earlier and later similar suggestions, but its influence likely was not great.

Yet Alexandrians were justly proud of the conference. It was the largest assembly of royal governors ever held in the colonies, and it would not be until 1774, when the Continental Congress met in Philadelphia, that another broad assembly of such influential colony representatives gathered to discuss their future.

Braddock's mission, however, proved to be a disaster. By April 27, Braddock and his army had left Alexandria, and on July 9, 1755, after a long and difficult march and only ten miles short of their objective, Fort Duquesne, they were routed by a smaller number of French and Indians. Over 65% of the British engaged were killed or wounded, and General Braddock himself was killed. The Virginia troops were hit particularly hard. Of three companies of Virginians, not more than 30 men still lived. One of those killed was Sergeant Thomas Longdon of Alexandria.

Young George Washington, who earlier had resigned his commission in the Virginia forces, accompanied Braddock as a volunteer aide. He survived unharmed, but during the

The April 2010 re-enactment of General Braddock welcoming royal governors to a conference he hosted at John Carlyle's house 255 years earlier to plan the first major campaign of the French and Indian War.
PHOTOGRAPH BY TED PULLIAM.

battle, two horses were shot out from under him and four bullets tore holes in his coat.

Braddock and his men had made a poor impression on Alexandrians. John Carlyle wrote that "they used us Like an Enemy Country & Took everything they wanted & paid Nothing or Very little for it." (This was not to be the only time in its history that Alexandria was treated harshly by an unfriendly army.)

Alexandrians were ahead of other colonists in experiencing the arrogance of British soldiers. But they and others throughout the colonies had learned that the British could be defeated—knowledge that would have its effect in the future.

THE TOWN EXPANDS AND ENTERTAINS

In October 1759, Andrew Burnaby, Vicar of Greenwich, England, stopped in Alexandria during his tour of the middle colonies and described the town as "a small trading place in one of the finest situations imaginable…. The town is built upon an arc of this [large circular] bay; at one extremity of which is a wharf; at the other a dock for building ships; with water sufficiently deep to launch a vessel of any rate or magnitude."

The wharf he mentioned was built by Fairfax County at the public area at West's Point just before General Braddock's forces arrived. The shipbuilding operation was that

Above: The Alexandria waterfront as it probably appeared c. 1760-1775.

Below: A section of the Carlyle-Dalton wharf excavated in 1982 by Alexandria Archaeology. It was re-buried and now is underneath the south side of the 100 block of Cameron Street.

of Thomas Fleming at Point Lumley at the foot of Duke Street, the first of many Alexandria shipbuilding enterprises.

The public wharf soon was joined by the first private wharf in the town, that of Carlyle & Dalton extending out from John Carlyle's property in late 1759 or early 1760. Carlyle & Dalton continued to prosper. Each man also, like many other Alexandrians, from time to time formed partnerships with other business-men, pooling their capital for a particular ven-ture, such as importing slaves, rum, or sugar. (There was as yet no bank in all of Virginia.)

Alexandria had its share of smaller business-es also, like that of dyer Paul Irmill, who took in "great quantities of woolen, Cloths, Stockings, yarn in hanks, and also all Kind of Linnens, Silks, and Brocades for Ladies vel-vets," according to court documents and who posted a black spaniel hunting dog at the door of his shop to "defend the said Cloths from Thieves and Robbers."

Alexandria was not all business and civic affairs. On February 15, 1760, George Washington, age twenty-seven, recorded in his diary attending a ball in Alexandria where there was music, dancing, and "in a conven-ient Room detached for the purpose abound-ed great plenty of Bread and Butter, some Biscuets with Tea, & Coffee," and he named this entertainment "the Bread & Butter Ball."

In 1761 Alexandrians selected the gregari-ous William Ramsay its honorary Lord Mayor, decorating him with a golden chain and per-suading him to lead a "grand procession" com-posed of "Sword and Mace bearers" and "many gentlemen of the town and country, wearing blue sashes." Bands played, and ships in the harbor flew banners. After the procession,

according to the *Maryland Gazette*, came a brilliant ball, a "sumptuous repast," and "fire-works, bonfires, and other demonstrations."

Alexandrians continued to improve their "finest situation imaginable." In 1759, a one and a half story brick town hall was built on Market Square not far from the courthouse, and in 1760, room was found on its lower floor for a school. In November 1762 the General Assembly authorized the expansion of Alexandria by a street to the south (Wolfe), a street to the west (Pitt), and 58 new lots. The trustees auctioned the new lots on May 9, 1763, to many willing bidders.

In the 1760s, Alexandrians began export-ing quantities of flour and wheat, and by 1775 they exported more flour and wheat than tobacco, diversifying their trade and foreshadowing real prosperity. But before Alexandria prospered, it needed to survive the cataclysm of the American Revolution.

CHAPTER III
THE AMERICAN REVOLUTION
1765-1782

REVOLUTION APPROACHES

On March 22, 1765, the British Parliament and George III enacted the Stamp Act requiring revenue stamps costing from a few pence to several pounds to be affixed to almost all printed documents in the colonies—law pleadings, bills of lading, newspapers, deeds, even playing cards. The act's purpose was to raise funds to defray the expenses of defending the colonies. Instead, it became the first giant step leading to the American Revolution.

When a session of the General Assembly began in Williamsburg on May 1, the old leaders of the House of Burgesses were uncertain what to do about the act's threat to the colonies. As a result, they dealt with other matters. By late May the session was almost over, and some burgesses, probably including George Washington, then a burgess for Frederick County (Winchester), had gone home.

Those staying included George Johnston, a burgess from Fairfax County, an Alexandrian (his home was at 224 South Lee Street), and a first class lawyer. At 65 he was somewhat old to be a revolutionary, but on May 29, with only about a third of the Assembly still present, Johnston moved that the House of Burgesses begin consideration of resolutions opposing the Stamp Act, resolutions that he, young Patrick Henry, and two other Burgesses had drafted. Patrick Henry seconded the motion.

During the next two days' impassioned debate on the resolutions, Patrick Henry is reported to have said: "Caesar had his Brutus, Charles the First had his Cromwell, and George the Third…." "Treason," shouted the Speaker. "…may profit by their example."

Henry then concluded, "If this be treason, make the most of it."

The House of Burgesses passed four anti-Stamp Act resolutions, although the three most incendiary resolutions of the seven drafted were defeated or not offered. Alexandrian George Johnston's contribution to the debate was key. Thomas Jefferson, then a law student, stood at the

George Johnston.
COURTESY OF THE FAIRFAX COUNTY PUBLIC LIBRARY
PHOTOGRAPHIC ARCHIVES.

door of the Assembly listening to the debate. About George Johnston's role he later wrote: "by him the learning and the logic of the case were chiefly maintained."

Later, however, all seven of the Virginia Resolutions were printed in northern colonial newspapers as though all had been adopted, including one resolution not even offered that read: "Resolved, That any person who shall… assert or maintain that any person or persons other than the General Assembly of this Colony have any right or authority to lay or impose any tax whatever on the inhabitants thereof, shall be deemed an enemy to this His Majesty's colony."

People in other colonies read of Virginia's apparent boldness and were inspired to their own bold actions in opposition to the Stamp Act. As a result, in March 1766, Parliament repealed it. After the repeal, John Carlyle wrote his brother "nothing Appears but that our Mother Country intends well for us which we are Obliged to her for."

Carlyle's optimism was short lived. Still needing money and now wanting to stress its authority, Parliament in 1767 passed the Townshend Act duties on importing into the colonies items such as tea, wine, glass, lead, and quality paper. Although all the Townshend duties but that on tea were eventually repealed, that remaining duty led in December 1773 to colonists in Boston dressed as Indians boarding ships loaded with tea and dumping it into the harbor. In response, Britain angrily closed Boston Harbor, which in turn set in motion a chain of events in Virginia and Alexandria that had severe consequences.

VIRGINIA AND ALEXANDRIA RESPOND

The General Assembly was meeting in Williamsburg in May 1774 when it learned of Boston port's closing. The House of Burgesses, deeply impressed with "the great Dangers to be derived to British America" from the example of the closure, passed a resolution setting aside June 1 "as a Day of Fasting, Humiliation, and Prayer." The royal governor, John Murray, fourth earl of Dunmore, promptly and unexpectedly dismissed the House. Immediately most House members, including George Washington (elected a burgess

from Fairfax County when the out-spoken George Johnston became terminally ill), walked down the street to the Raleigh Tavern to plan their next steps. Among other actions, they decided to call a special convention in Virginia to be held on August 1. Washington later wrote "god only knows what is to become of us."

Meanwhile on May 29, 1774, a group of Alexandria citizens, probably as yet unaware of the happenings in Williamsburg but "deeply interested as we are, in the fate of Boston," formed a committee of correspondence to communicate with neighboring towns "in the most speedy manner" about the present "Alarming situation." The first three names on the list of members of the Alexandria committee were the three Fairfax Street neighbors, Carlyle, Dalton, and Ramsay.

Alexandria then had no newspaper. Alexandrians obtained information about the fate of Boston and the larger world generally through newspapers printed in Annapolis and Williamsburg, letters from friends, incoming ships' captains, stagecoach travelers, and now, semi-official correspondence with other towns. They discussed this information energetically, then and during the Revolution, on street corners, in churches (the new Christ Church had just been completed in 1773 and the Old Presbyterian Meeting House would be in 1775— almost as if Alexandrians built stable houses of worship to sustain their faith and themselves through the turmoil they sensed coming), and over a pipe of tobacco, a tankard of ale, or bowl of rum punch in taverns like Arell's on Market Square or the widow Hawkins' on Royal Street (near where Gadsby's Tavern stands today).

THE FAIRFAX RESOLVES

On July 14, 1774, Fairfax County elected George Washington and Charles Broadwater as its delegates to the Virginia Convention, chose Washington to head a committee to draft instructions for the delegates, and set July 18 as the date for the county to meet in Alexandria to discuss the instructions.

The night before the instructions were to be presented at Alexandria, Fairfax County resident George Mason stayed at Mount Vernon with Washington. It is generally agreed that

Mason was the lead drafter of what next day became the Fairfax Resolves. Mason, then 50 years old, and Washington, then 42, had known each other for years and had consulted frequently about farming techniques, served together as Alexandria trustees, and, in 1769, worked together on Virginia's first non-importation agreement.

The following morning the county met in Alexandria, probably in the courthouse on Market Square (which likely was packed with people). Washington, as chairman of the drafting committee, probably proposed the resolutions with comments in support that were short and to the point. (Thomas Jefferson wrote that he never heard Washington speak more than ten minutes at a time and then always "to the main point that was to decide the question.") After some discussion, his and Mason's resolutions, slightly amended, were adopted.

The adopted resolutions proposed that the colonies refuse to import most goods from Great Britain or to export certain American goods to Great Britain, and most importantly, that all colonies attend a congress to prepare "for the Defense and preservation of our Common rights." The resolutions also beseeched the king "not to reduce his faithful Subjects of America to a State of desperation, and to reflect, that from our Sovereign [the king], there can be but one Appeal." Although not stated explicitly, the only appeal remaining was war.

Of the several Virginia counties that proposed resolutions, Fairfax County's were "the most detailed, the most influential, and the most radical" according to historian Jeff Broadwater.

The meeting also appointed a county committee of 25, including Washington, Mason, Ramsay, Carlyle, and Dalton as well as John West, uncle of Hugh West of the Hunting Creek Warehouse, and two Alexanders, Philip and Charles, to address "any emergency."

Washington and Broadwater carried the Fairfax resolves to the Virginia Convention. As the resolves proposed, the Convention banned importing British goods and exporting goods to Great Britain, although the export ban would not become effective for a year. It also elected delegates, including George Washington, to the First Continental Congress meeting in Philadelphia in September.

Events quickly escalated. At a second Virginia Convention in March 1775, Patrick Henry gave his "give me liberty or give me death" speech; on April 19, Massachusetts minutemen and British regulars exchanged gunfire at Lexington and Concord; on June 8, royal governor Dunmore fled Williamsburg to a British warship off Yorktown; on June 16, at the Second Continental Congress, George Washington accepted the position of commander-in-chief of the Continental forces; and in the fall of 1775, Dunmore took control of Norfolk and offered freedom to any slave who joined him.

Following these momentous events, there appeared in the *Virginia Gazette* of December 22, 1775, a transcript of some very disturbing papers found on a loyalist, Major John Connolly, captured at a tavern near Hagerstown, Maryland. According to those papers, Connolly planned to gather a force of Ohio and Detroit Indians, backwoods loyalists, "serviceable French," and British soldiers and artillery, transport them from Detroit to Fort Pitt (earlier Fort Duquesne and now Pittsburgh), and march them down Braddock's Road to Alexandria (a Braddock's march in reverse). In Alexandria he would rendezvous with Governor Dunmore's ships and soldiers, and then, as one of his confederates wrote, "sweep all the Country before him."

Earlier, with Dunmore's approval, Connolly had sailed to Boston to obtain the approval of General Thomas Gage, commander-in-chief of

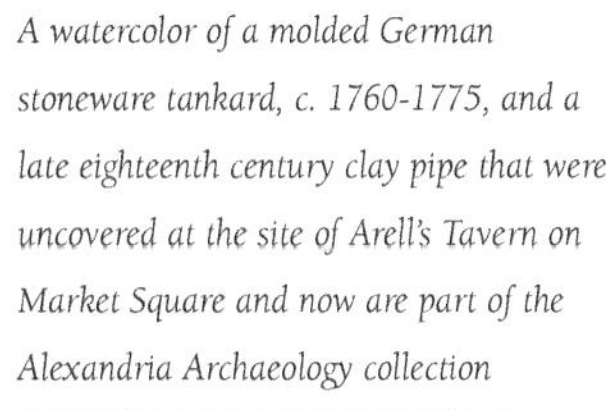

❖

A watercolor of a molded German stoneware tankard, c. 1760-1775, and a late eighteenth century clay pipe that were uncovered at the site of Arell's Tavern on Market Square and now are part of the Alexandria Archaeology collection
COURTESY OF TED PULLIAM. WATERCOLOR BY ERIK HOTTENSTEIN.

the British land forces. Gage was familiar with part of the route, having been with General Braddock in Alexandria and on the road to Fort Pitt (then Fort Duquesne), and he approved. Major Connolly was on his way to the back-country in disguise to execute his plan when he was captured. It was a long-shot scheme at best, and Connolly was an unlikely man to execute it successfully (one modern historian referred to him as "a local blowhard"), but its discovery unnerved Alexandrians.

Their uneasiness increased when a month later Dunmore, driven out of Norfolk to his ships, shelled the city, starting a fire that burned much of Norfolk to the ground. Alexandrians found themselves with nothing between them and the enemy but an open river and a company of militia armed mainly with clubs. As the Alexandrians wrote in December 1775: "The Sword is drawn, the Bayonet is already at our Breasts, therefore some immediate Effort is necessary to ward off the meditated Blow."

Lund Washington, George Washington's cousin who managed Mount Vernon in Washington's absence, on January 17, 1776, wrote Washington in Cambridge, Massachusetts: "The Alexandrians expect to have their Town burnt by the Enemy soon."

LOYALISTS

In such an atmosphere, Alexandrians were forced to choose sides. Were they with the mother country or with their home?

In December 1775, Alexandrian Enoch Hawksworth, not wanting to renounce his loyalty to king and country, "sold his goods, settled his debts, closed his store that stood on North Fairfax Street adjoining Col. John Carlyle's house," and sailed away from Alexandria "to become 'a wandering and forlorn Refugee,'" wrote author Marian Van Landingham.

He was not alone. In late 1776, Harry Piper, a tobacco agent in Alexandria for the firm of Dixon and Littledale of Whitehaven, England, left for his mother country. He had been an outstanding Alexandria citizen— bought a lot in the first auction in 1749, served as a town trustee, and even signed an early non-importation agreement—and his

letters make it clear that he had no real desire to leave. He knew, however, as he wrote his employer, once the Continental Congress's ban on exports to Great Britain, including tobacco, took effect (as it soon would), "my stay here can neither be of advantage to you or agreeable to me." So he sailed away.

Members of the Fairfax family each made his or her own decision. Old Lord Fairfax, 82 in 1775, continued to live unmolested west of Winchester, "a silent, inactive bystander" as a biographer recorded, until his death in December 1781. His old land agent, William Fairfax, had died in 1757. William's son, and George Washington's great friend, George William Fairfax, and his wife Sarah had gone to England in 1773 to deal with the family estate and see doctors. They never returned.

THE DEFENSE OF ALEXANDRIA

The defense of Alexandria and the Potomac River was such a concern that George Washington wrote in November 1775 from Massachusetts to William Ramsay (Ramsay and Washington were close—Washington even helped support Ramsay's son William at "the Jersey College," now Princeton) asking Ramsay to investigate places along the Potomac where derelict ships could be sunk and shore batteries erected to block the passage of British warships. Ramsay investigated, but unfortunately

❖

Patrick Henry delivering his speech before the House of Burgesses in May 1765 in which he said: "If this be treason, make the most of it."

COURTESY OF THE LIBRARY OF CONGRESS. PAINTING BY PETER FREDERICK ROTHERMEL.

found that the channel was too deep and the river too wide for that to be practical.

At the urging of Alexandrians Carlyle, Dalton, Ramsay, and others, however, Virginia's revolutionary government furnished them funds to buy three armed ships, build two row galleys (fairly small sailing vessels with oars, thick gunwales, and several cannons), and equip them for use on the Potomac against "Lord Dunmore's Pirates."

The government placed George Mason and John Dalton in charge of the vessels' acquisition. Mason was ill and rarely left Gunston Hall, so it fell to Dalton to do most of the work. Mason wrote of Dalton: "He is a steady diligent Man, & without such Assistance I could not have undertaken it [procuring and building the vessels]." Ships, including one called the *American Congress*, were bought but finding gunpowder, cannon, even sail cloth for them and for the galleys proved difficult. By May 1776, however, a spy for Dunmore reported the vessels were mostly ready and were "fully Manned with desperadoes."

In an effort to remedy the shortage of gunpowder, muskets, and ammunition, Alexandrian Robert Townshend Hooe, his business partner from Maryland, Daniel of St. Thomas Jennifer, and a young future Alexandrian, Richard Harrison, developed contacts with the French in Martinique and opened up a channel of supply, trading Alexandrian flour and bread for French arms. Dodging British ships was dangerous, but ships chartered by Jennifer and Hooe, like the sloop *Molly*, were successful enough to help the patriot cause.

In late July 1776, Alexandrians had a scare when Dunmore's ships came up the Potomac searching for fresh water. Just below Dumfries the British burned several buildings and routed a militia unit but sailed no further upriver.

Many Alexandrians did not wait for the British to come to them. Men from Alexandria with names like Arell, West, Conway, and Lynn served in Virginia regiments and fought from Massachusetts to South Carolina. Alexandrian Robert Hanson Harrison served for five years as an aide to Washington. John Fitzgerald of Alexandria was another Washington aide. Doctor James Craik, who had been with General Braddock, was Chief Physician and Surgeon of the Continental Army. Alexandrian Lieutenant Colonel Charles Simms succeeded Colonel James Hendricks, also of Alexandria, as second-in-command of the 6th Virginia Infantry regiment when Hendricks became commander of the 1st. Moreover, fifteen-year-old George William Carlyle, John Carlyle's only son, was killed in South Carolina only three weeks before the Battle of Yorktown.

Finally, in early August 1776, Dunmore sailed away from the Chesapeake for New York. His leaving did not mean Alexandria was free to resume its usual shipping. At unpredictable times British warships appeared at the mouth of the bay and seized vessels leaving and coming, much to Alexandria's and all Virginia's detriment.

ESCAPE AND ATTACK

On May 1, 1777, a notice appeared in the *Maryland Gazette* offering a reward of $100 for apprehending nine Loyalist prisoners who had escaped from the Alexandria jail. Aiding their escape was Nicholas Cresswell, a young Englishman who had come to Alexandria to seek his fortune. Seven of the escapees made their way to a British warship in the Delaware Bay, but two, discouraged earlier, returned to Alexandria. There the two hoped to help their cause by accusing six townsmen of planning to burn the town and murder its inhabitants.

The six accused Alexandrians, including

❖

A scene in the yard of Christ Church after Sunday services, c. 1775.

THE CENTURY MAGAZINE, NOVEMBER 1887

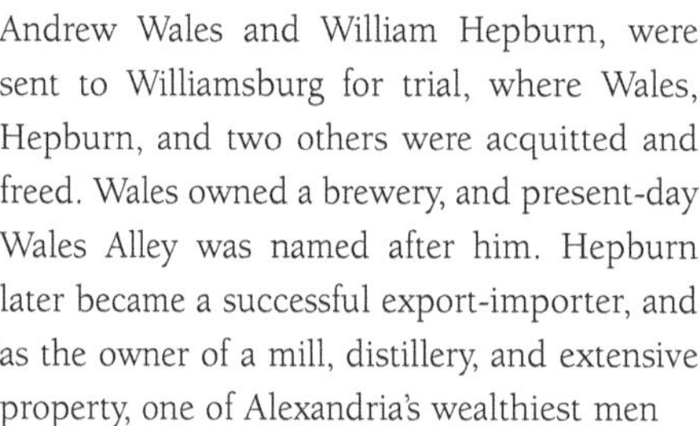

❖

Above: John Murray, fourth earl of Dunmore, the last royal governor of Virginia, copied from the original by Joshua Reynolds.

COURTESY OF THE VIRGINIA HISTORICAL SOCIETY.

Below: The home of successful Alexandria merchant Robert Townshend Hooe, who helped Alexandria obtain powder and muskets during the Revolution, was the first mayor of Alexandria, and was one of the justices of the peace whose appointment led to the famous Supreme Court case of Marbury v. Madison. This house at 200 Prince Street and 201 South Lee Street was built c. 1780. Its second floor parlor was sold during the Great Depression to a St. Louis museum, but a replica of the parlor is on display at the Lyceum in Alexandria.

PHOTOGRAPH BY TED PULLIAM.

Andrew Wales and William Hepburn, were sent to Williamsburg for trial, where Wales, Hepburn, and two others were acquitted and freed. Wales owned a brewery, and present-day Wales Alley was named after him. Hepburn later became a successful export-importer, and as the owner of a mill, distillery, and extensive property, one of Alexandria's wealthiest men

Alexandrians' last and closest brush with combat came in the spring of 1781 when a British sloop of war, the *Savage*, came to Mount Vernon and seized a boat and 17 slaves. Martha Washington was not present then, and it is not clear whether the British knew to whom Mount Vernon belonged.

Lund Washington, General Washington's cousin and estate manager, went on board the *Savage* with refreshments in an effort to regain the Washington property. The only thing his visit accomplished, however, was to infuriate the General when he heard about it. Washington wrote Lund that rather than giving those "plundering scoundrels" refreshments, "it would have been less painful" to him if "they had burnt my House, and laid my Plantation in ruins."

In the dark early morning only days later, a British vessel, probably the *Savage*, sailed into Alexandria harbor. There its men boarded a vessel from Baltimore loaded with tobacco, confined the vessel's seamen, and prepared to sail her down river. At this point, men on a nearby vessel discovered them and gave the alarm. The British immediately abandoned the Baltimore ship, climbed into a boat alongside, rowed back to their own ship, and sailed hurriedly back down river. However, an armed schooner pursued and captured them at Boyd's Hole off King George County. Alexandria's defenses finally had been tested and had proven effective.

THE BRITISH VANQUISHED

At Yorktown in October 1781, Washington's Continentals, Count Rochambeau's French army, and Count de Grasse's French navy eliminated the British from Virginia for good. The following July, Rochambeau's soldiers marching back north camped just outside Alexandria.

There, as an observer reported, "the most elegant and handsome young ladies of the neighborhood" danced with the French officers "in the middle of the camp, to the sound of military music; and…the circle was in a great measure composed of soldiers, who, from the heat of the weather, had disengaged themselves from their clothes, retaining not an article of dress except their shirts, which in general were neither extremely long, nor in the best condition; nor did this occasion the least embarrassment to the ladies, many of whom were of highly polished manners, and the most exquisite delicacy; or to their friends or parents."

Perhaps through their dancing, these young Alexandrians celebrated the freedom and release they now felt after the stifling British threat had ended.

CHAPTER IV

THE GOLDEN AGE
1783-1799

The Revolutionary War formally ended with the Peace of Paris signed in 1783. Alexandria then grew rapidly in almost every way—in population, geographical expanse, variety of businesses, new institutions, number of brick buildings, and sophistication of its governmental structure.

By the end of the century Alexandria was no longer "a small trading place" as the good Vicar Burnaby described it in 1759. It was not even the same as General Washington found it in December 1783 when he returned to Alexandria from the war (welcomed by a huge feast and the firing of thirteen cannons).

The most obvious change was on the waterfront. The effort to push the town out into the Potomac begun by the Carlyle-Dalton wharf had been greatly expanded. Alexandrians built additional wharves and used dirt obtained from leveling the bluffs to fill in the bay's shallow tidal flats, a process called "banking out," to reach the river channel that ran between the two points, West's Point and Point Lumley. By the mid 1780s the two ends of Water Street had been joined in the middle and Union Street had been added along the waterfront. By the beginning of the new century, the waterfront was a curve no longer but a rough straight line, as it is today.

Not only had the width of the waterfront increased but also its business. New warehouses sprang up, like the four-story granite and brick warehouse built around 1796 by John Fitzgerald at the southeast corner of King and Union Streets. From these warehouses, wharves stretched out into the river, and beside the wharves bobbing up and down were tall-masted schooners, sloops, brigs, snows, and larger vessels—a few built in Alexandria at John Hunter's boatyard. Lund Washington wrote in 1790: "[T]he port of Alexandria has seldom less than 20 Square Rigged Sale of Vessels in it and often many more."

❖

Gadsby's Tavern, later known as City Hotel, c. the early 1920s, looking south from the intersection of Cameron and Royal Streets. The tavern consists of the two buildings on the southwest corner of the intersection. The older building is the smaller one on the left.
COURTESY OF THE ALEXANDRIA LIBRARY, SPECIAL COLLECTIONS, MORRIS LOEB COLLECTION.

Above: The Fitzgerald Warehouse, c. 1937. The warehouse was built by John Fitzgerald at the southeast corner of King and Union Streets. At the far left is King Street and at the right is Wales Alley.

COURTESY OF THE LIBRARY OF CONGRESS.

Below: A shipping ad placed in the Alexandria Gazette in 1785 by the firm of Hooe and Harrison advertising merchandise imported into the port of Alexandria. The firm's store was at the corner of Duke Street and The Strand at 10 Duke Street. Osnaburgs, duck, cambricks, and lawns were types of cloth.

COURTESY OF THE ALEXANDRIA LIBRARY,
SPECIAL COLLECTIONS.

Ships sailed from Alexandria to Europe, the West Indies, and coastal America. They still carried tobacco, but more and more often their holds were filled with Indian corn, wheat, and flour, particularly flour. Alexandria was an official Virginia flour inspection station, and flour merchants maintained offices in town and partnerships with mills further west. Wagon after wagon traveled the dirt roads from Fauquier, Loudon, and Prince William Counties to Alexandria's waterfront. There they off-loaded cargoes of flour, wheat, rye, and corn to be carried by slaves on board ships and sent abroad.

Ships returning to Alexandria brought wine, raisins, olive oil, nuts, and straw mats from Spain; dessert wines from Portugal; pins, frocks, cloth, and an array of manufactured goods from England; quills, artificial flowers, and tiles from Holland; and rum, oranges, brown and white sugar, turtles, and coffee from the West Indies, according to historian Betty Harrington Macdonald. Some of these goods were carried by smaller boats to local ports along the coast, but much was sold out of waterfront stores. Merchant and shipping firms bore Alexandria names like Hooe & Harrison, Herbert, Harper, Ramsay, Conway, Hartshorne, Muir, and Adam. Although economic prosperity was uneven during this period, by 1795, according to historian T. Michael Miller, Alexandria ranked as the seventh largest seaport in the United States and the third largest exporter of flour.

The increase in shipping was due partly to the General Assembly's appointing Alexandria an international port of entry in 1779. In the early 1780s, Charles Lee, brother of General Light Horse Harry Lee and future uncle of Robert E. Lee, was the town's first customs officer and maintained a customs office at 305 Cameron Street.

THE NEW STATES MEET

After the Revolution, however, this prosperity was threatened by a conflict between Virginia and Maryland concerning who regulated trade on the Potomac. Maryland claimed jurisdiction over the entire width of the Potomac River, from bank to bank, under its 1632 charter from King Charles I, a claim Virginia contested. Both states appointed commissioners to resolve the issue and scheduled a meeting for Alexandria in March 1785. Thus began a series of meetings that step by step led to the convention in Philadelphia that wrote the U.S. Constitution.

The Maryland commissioners arrived in Alexandria on time, but there had been a mixup in notifying the Virginia commissioners of their appointment. No Virginian was there to meet them. Again at a key time, George Washington acted. Learning of the situation, he sent his carriage to one of the Virginia commissioners, George Mason, and conveyed him to Alexandria. There Mason rounded up another Virginia commissioner, Alexander Henderson, an Alexandria and Dumfries merchant, and they promptly met with the Marylanders (possibly in Gadsby's Tavern). It was cold, however, and snowing, and Washington soon invited them all to the more comfortable Mount Vernon. There the two states' commissioners signed a compact guaranteeing free navigation of the Potomac.

The meeting was so successful that Maryland and Virginia agreed to meet again in Annapolis in early September 1786 and invited all the former colonies to join them to discuss regulating interstate trade.

Only five states attended the Annapolis meeting, but the delegates from those states were acutely aware of the weakness of Congress under the Articles of Confederation, the interstate agreement under which the country was governed. The meeting ended with the delegates noting "the embarrassments which characterize the present state of our national affairs"

Hooe and Harrison,
Have for Sale at their Store,
OSnaburgs, Ravens duck, brown rolls, Russia duck, Holland's ditto, white-lead, red ditto, Spanish brown, red ochre, yellow ditto, white vitriol, verdigrease, brimstone, sand-glasses, spyglasses, sheet-lead, sheet-copper, German steel, loglines, deepsea ditto, houseline, marline, hamberline, sail twine, seine ditto, sheet-tin in boxes, steel wire, tar, turpentine, English and Dutch cordage, anchors of different sizes, mould candles, Hyson, bohea and souchong tea, black pepper, single refined and double refined sugar, candied ditto, gin in cases, muskets, butter pots, water pitchers, queen's china, glass ware, delf bowls, long and short pipes, violins, looking-glasses, hatchets, carpenters' and joiners' tools, scythes, bolting-cloths, blankets, flannels, hats, cotton stockings, yarn and worsted ditto, diaper napkins, cambricks, lawns, check shirts, gauze handkerchiefs, old hock in bottles, &c.
Alexandria, Jan. 26, 1785.

and issuing a ringing call for a convention of all states in Philadelphia in May 1787 to address concerns about the national government. That convention produced the Constitution.

ALEXANDRIA'S DIFFERENT LOOK

In the meantime, in October 1785, the General Assembly authorized Alexandria to extend its town limits to Great Hunting Creek in the south, Four Mile Run to the north, and one mile from Market Square to the west. By 1798, as shown on George Gilpin's map of that year, the town had established or planned new streets westward across Washington Street to both sides of West Street, northward to Montgomery Street, and south all the way to Great Hunting Creek.

The appearance of the town itself also had changed. By the mid-1790s many of the dirt streets were paved with cobblestones. There were new brick buildings, such as a new Market House on Market Square built in 1785 and the Gadsby's Tavern buildings (the smaller, Georgian building to the south built around 1785, and the larger Federal-style north building built in 1792). New churches were constructed—the first Methodist church was built in Chapel Alley in 1791 and St. Mary's Catholic Chapel completed near the present Washington Street entrance to St. Mary's Cemetery around 1796. New houses were constructed, like the Lee-Fendall House in 1785. A visitor to Alexandria in 1795 was struck by "the vast number of houses which I saw building as we passed through the street. The number of people employed as carpenters and masons. The hammer and trowel were at work everywhere...."

New institutions were started, such as Alexandria's first newspaper, *The Virginia Journal & Alexandria Advertiser* in 1784 (later known by various names but referred to below as the *Alexandria Gazette*). The cornerstone was laid in 1785 for the Alexandria Academy, a "Seminary of learning" for the children of Alexandria. The Alexandria Masonic Lodge was chartered by the Grand Lodge of Virginia in 1788. The Stabler-Leadbeater Apothecary Shop first opened its doors in 1792. The Alexandria Library Company was founded as a subscription library

(annual fee $4) in 1794. The first fire company, the Friendship Volunteer Fire Company, had been started in 1774, and by 1799, there were four fire companies in Alexandria. But perhaps most important for Alexandria traders and merchants—the Bank of Alexandria, the first bank in Virginia, was chartered in 1792.

Alexandria could boast of a variety of businesses, like a ropewalk owned by Samuel Harper near Washington and King Streets, which consisted of a low building some twelve hundred feet long inside which a man walked backward spinning fibers into rope and paying the rope out as he walked. Also in Alexandria were coopers, such as George Hill, who rented a space off Water Street to make barrels, nail kegs, buckets, etc.; potters like Henry Piercy at the northeast corner of Duke and Washington Streets; and silversmiths like Adam Lynn, Jr., on King Street, who in 1796 advertised "all kinds of gold and silver work, such as coffee pots, tea pots, cream pots, sugar dishes, salts, spoons, etc." Commercial bakers like James Adam provided seamen with ship bread, and John Fitzgerald, Andrew Wales, and James Kerr operated breweries.

With all of this activity, the population of Alexandria in 1790 was 2,748, including 543 slaves and 52 free black men and women. By 1800 it had risen to 4,971. Some of the slaves and free blacks were trained artisans who, along with others, did the "hammer and trowel" work on the new buildings. The population also included Quakers, who had been persecuted in the northern colonies for their pacifism and began arriving during the Revolution after the passage of the Virginia Declaration of Rights in 1776.

NEW GOVERNMENTS, NEW LEADERS

On October 4, 1779, Virginia replaced the Alexandria trustees with a new form of city government, a mayor-council system. Twelve members of a board of aldermen and common council were elected by voters, and they selected the mayor from among themselves.

The town also had new leaders. John Dalton and John Carlyle had died before the end of the Revolution, and William Ramsay died in 1785. The new mayors were men like Robert

❖

This house at 220 South Lee Street is called a "flounder house" because, like the fish, it has a flat side on the property line that has no "eyes" (windows). Built mainly in the late 1700s and early 1800s, flounders were ideal for Alexandria's deep but narrow lots, and sometimes were built back from the front property line as a temporary home until the owner could acquire enough money to build a nicer house in front, at which time the flounder became the typical service ell for the main house. Occasionally, that main house was never built.

Above: A large slip-decorated earthenware dish (actual diameter 13 inches) found in a privy behind Henry Piercy's retail shop in the 400 block of King Street. The "slip," a mixture of clay and water, was applied to the dish using a cup and hollow quills, somewhat like applying decorative icing to a cake.

COURTESY OF CERAMICS IN AMERICAN AND ALEXANDRIA ARCHAEOLOGY. PHOTOGRAPH BY GAVIN ASHWORTH.

Below: Dr. Elisha Cullen Dick

COURTESY OF THE ALEXANDRIA LIBRARY SPECIAL COLLECTIONS, OUR TOWN COLLECTION. PAINTING ATTRIBUTED TO WILLIAM WILLIAMS

Townshend Hooe, Colonel James Hendricks, Richard Conway, John Fitzgerald, and Dennis Ramsay, son of William Ramsay, many of whom had served in the Revolution or aided the patriot cause as civilians.

April 15, 1791, was the symbolic beginning of perhaps an even greater change in the governmental structure of Alexandria. At Jones Point on that date was laid the first cornerstone of the new District of Columbia in which Alexandria was to be included, effective in 1801. (The work of surveying the district had begun earlier, in February, also at Jones Point, with the assistance of Benjamin Banneker, the sixty-year-old son of a white woman and a black slave. Largely self-taught, he had become an excellent astronomer and surveyor.)

Officiating at the cornerstone ceremony were two of the three commissioners who were to supervise construction of the federal city, accompanied by Alexandria's mayor, aldermen, and councilmen. Offerings of corn, wine, and oil were laid atop the stone in a Masonic ritual symbolizing nourishment, refreshment, and joy. Earlier at Wise's Tavern in Alexandria, the company had raised a glass of wine and offered an optimistic toast: "May the Stone which we are about to place in the ground remain an immoveable monument of the wisdom and unanimity of North America."

THE FUN SIDE OF ALEXANDRIA

Not everything about Alexandria was serious, however. Alexandria's first theater was built in 1799 at 406 Cameron Street. (Only the year before a company of players from Philadelphia were forced to act in a nearby barn.)

Native Alexandrians knew how to entertain agreeably. The young Dr. Elisha Cullen Dick, who was skillful on several musical instruments and sang "with great power and sweetness," once sent a dinner invitation that began:

> If you can eat a good fat duck,
> Come with us and take pot luck.
> Of white ducks we have a pair
> So plump, so round, so fat, so fair,
> A London Alderman would fight
> Through pies and tarts to get a bite.

At least one visitor thought Alexandria had gone too far in its modes of entertainment. A strait-laced carpenter passing through town, wrote: "Alexandria is one of the most wicked places I ever beheld in my life; cockfighting, horse racing, with every species of gambling and cheating, being apparently the principal business going forward. As a proof of this, you may judge of the extent of this dissipation when I inform you, this little place contains no less than between forty and fifty billiard tables...."

GEORGE WASHINGTON

When George Washington returned to Mount Vernon in 1783, he planned to stay there. Yet in 1789, without campaigning, he was elected President of the United States. An overflow crowd of Alexandrians at Wise's Tavern at the northeast corner of Cameron and North Fairfax Streets sent him off with heart-felt speeches. Washington, to his embarrassment, needed more than speeches. He had to borrow money from a former mayor of Alexandria, Richard Conway, to pay his debts in Virginia before leaving for New York, then the U.S. capital, in order to assume the presidency.

Eight years later George Washington returned to Mount Vernon, and, on December 14, 1799, he died there. In this last illness, he was attended by three doctors, two of whom were Alexandrians: Dr. James Craik, his old friend from French and Indian War days, and Dr. Elisha Cullen Dick. A month before his death, on November 17, Washington attended church in Alexandria, his last visit to the town.

He was buried at Mount Vernon on December 18, with Alexandria town officers and many Alexandrians attending. In the funeral oration delivered to the U.S. Congress and other mourners in Philadelphia, Washington's dashing and controversial Revolutionary War general Light Horse Harry Lee, future Alexandria resident and future father of Robert E. Lee, said of Washington: "First in war, first in peace, and first in the hearts of his countrymen."

The new nineteenth century began for Alexandria without George Washington but with the hope of increased prosperity as part of the new District of Columbia.

ALEXANDRIA, DISTRICT OF COLUMBIA
1801-1847

THE SUPREME COURT, ALEXANDRIANS, AND THE LEES OF VIRGINIA

Officially Alexandria became part of the new District of Columbia on February 27, 1801, much to the joy of Alexandrians, who believed that their inclusion in the new capital area would expand their success of the previous decade.

Time would tell, but almost immediately inclusion in the new District led to the involvement of Alexandrians, including a member of the distinguished Lee family, in one of the most famous court cases in U.S. history.

In March 1801, during the last hours of John Adams's presidency, Adams signed and sealed commissions naming three prominent Alexandrians: Robert Townshend Hooe, William Harper, and Dennis Ramsay, and one Georgetowner, William Marbury, justices of the peace in the newly created District of Columbia. The commissions, however, were undelivered when Thomas Jefferson took office. President Jefferson then refused to deliver the commissions, and the four almost-justices-of-the-peace filed suit to compel him to deliver them..

The case, *Marbury v. Madison*, came before the Supreme Court, and Chief Justice John Marshall delivered the court's opinion. In that opinion for the first time the court invalidated a law passed by Congress and signed by the President as being contrary to the Constitution. As Marshall wrote: "It is emphatically the province and duty of the Judicial Department [and by implication, not that of the Congress or the President] to say what the law is."

Arguing the case on behalf of the plaintiffs was Charles Lee, a member of the prominent Lee clan. He had settled in Alexandria late in the last century and had served as a Potomac River customs officer then as Attorney General of the United States under both Washington and Adams.

❖

The tide lock of the Alexandria Canal at the foot of First Street during the Civil War.

Above: Charles Lee.
COURTESY OF ALEXANDRIA LIBRARY, SPECIAL
COLLECTIONS, OUR TOWN COLLECTION. PAINTING
POSSIBLY BY CEPHAS THOMPSON.

Below: Robert E. Lee's boyhood home, 607
Oronoco Street, c. the 1870s or 1880s.
COURTESY OF THE ALEXANDRIA LIBRARY, SPECIAL
COLLECTIONS, WILLIAM F. SMITH COLLECTION.

With his wife, Anne Lee, who was also his cousin, Charles was the first of what would become a community of Lees living in Alexandria. (Charles Lee briefly rented the Lloyd House then moved to 407 North Washington Street.) Following him to Alexandria were three brothers, a sister, and several cousins. They established a small enclave on the 400 block of North Washington Street and 600 block of Oronoco. Charles' sister, Mary Lee Fendall, lived in the Lee-Fendall house, at 614 Oronoco, with husband Richard Fendall, also a Lee descendant. The fifth generation of a family that had prospered in Virginia since the mid-1600s, the Lees brought to Alexandria a new touch of elegance.

One of Charles's brothers was General Henry "Light Horse Harry" Lee, who moved to Alexandria in 1810 with his second wife, Ann Carter Lee, and their four children, including three-year-old Robert Edward Lee. (The family lived first at what is now 611 Cameron Street, then moved to 607 Oronoco Street.)

Unfortunately, few firsthand accounts of Robert Lee's childhood in Alexandria exist. However, his older brother Carter had "vivid recollections of [his own] boyhood spent trapping squirrels and rabbits, stealing the neighbors' apples, playing 'marbles, hopscotch….'" activities that Robert likely shared, as Robert's biographer Elizabeth Brown Pryor wrote. Also, Robert undoubtedly felt at home among the warm community of Alexandria Lees.

His childhood, however, also had its darker side. His father General Harry Lee had been a soldier and a hero in the Revolution who fought with George Washington. Afterward, however, he was constantly and heavily in debt. In 1813, to escape his numerous creditors and ease his spirits, Harry Lee sailed to the West Indies, leaving Robert without a father and his family virtually without funds. Five years later, the general died on his way home to Alexandria.

In a letter home, the elder Lee had written about his youngest son: "Robert was always good, and will be confirmed in his happy turn of mind by his ever-watchful and affectionate mother." That turned out to be true.

Robert Lee was educated at the Alexandria Academy and at Quaker Benjamin Hallowell's fine school at 609 Oronoco Street. In July 1825, he left Alexandria to enter West Point.

WAR COMES TO TOWN

The evening of August 27, 1814, men and women standing silently on wharves on the Alexandria waterfront could look north and see the smoke rising from the remains of the Capitol burned by the now-departed British soldiers and at the same time hear from the south the even more disturbing sounds of cannon fire. Although the British Army that caused so much suffering in Washington had neglected them, they realized they might not be so lucky with the British Navy sailing up the Potomac River from the south.

The sound of cannons came from Fort Warburton (now Fort Washington), six miles down river from Alexandria on the Maryland side, as it was being attacked by a squadron of British ships under Captain James Gordon that included two frigates, a rocket ship, and three bomb vessels. The fort was the last obstacle to the British on the Potomac. Soon their way would be clear to sail on to Alexandria.

In Alexandria no one remained to defend the citizens but about one hundred overaged, sick, or unreliable men left after authorities in Washington had ordered the town's militia elsewhere. Even the Washington authorities themselves—military commanders, heads of governmental departments, and the president himself—were now scattered about the countryside.

Two days later, August 29, Alexandrians awoke to find the squadron with its 128 guns anchored in the harbor "but a few hundred yards from the wharves, and the houses so situated that they might have been laid in ashes in a few minutes," the Common Council later wrote.

Captain Gordon promised he would not destroy the town nor molest its inhabitants, if the Americans would not commence hostilities. Further, the Alexandrians must surrender all military stores, all shipping in the harbor, and all merchandise in town intended for export. Having no option, the Council agreed to his terms, and the British promptly began removing ships and merchandise while dejected Alexandria merchants stood by "viewing with melancholy countenance the British sailors gutting their warehouses of their contents," one observer wrote.

On September 1, Gordon's well-loaded ships began to leave Alexandria and sail back down the Potomac. Their journey down river, however, was contested, finally, by American forces under naval Captain David Porter, including the Alexandria militia. Porter placed his men and cannons on the hastily fortified heights four miles below Mount Vernon at Belvoir, the old William Fairfax estate (now Fort Belvoir). From there for five days they battled the British ships headed down river. Even though they sunk no ships, the Alexandrians and other Americans fought well. Eleven Americans were killed and 19 wounded, while Americans killed seven British and wounded 35.

Alexandria was free then from further harm, but its decision to surrender rather than fight made it for a while an object of national scorn.

NEW MERCHANT GENTRY

In plundering Alexandria, the British took, according to Alexandrians, "three ships, three brigs, several bay and river craft" plus about 1,000 hogsheads of tobacco, 150 bales of cotton, some $5,000 worth of wine, sugar, and other articles, and around 16,000 barrels of flour—substantial losses. Gradually, however, resilient Alexandrians recovered.

Helping to overcome these setbacks was the heavy demand for flour in the West Indies, in England, and for British troops fighting Napoleon in Portugal and Spain. In fact, in 1817 Alexandria reached its high point in quantity of flour exported—more than 217,000 barrels.

In 1817 the town contained, according to historian Harold Hurst, "512 brick and 383 frame three-story and two-story residences and warehouses; 429 one-story and one-half story houses" plus churches, schools, bake houses, shipyards, ropewalks, and sheds for blacksmiths, cabinetmakers, tanners, and other artisans. Two sugar refineries, one in the 100 block of North Alfred Street and the second in the 200 block of North Washington Street, were probably Alexandria's most valuable manufacturing plants during the early 1800's. From 1800 to 1820, Alexandria's population almost doubled, from 4,971 to 8,218.

Construction of the Little River Turnpike from 1803 to 1819 provided Alexandria for the first time with a well-built link to Western Virginia, the primary source of Alexandria's wheat and flour. The waterfront continued to be Alexandria's main center of economic activity, yet opening the turnpike led also to the development of a second such center, the vibrant community called West End, located west of Hooff's Run and south of Shuter's Hill just outside Alexandria's then boundaries. The community took its name from John West, who subdivided his property there in 1796. It served teamsters who drove wagon loads of wheat and

❖

Above: General Henry "Light Horse Harry" Lee.

Below: On August 24, 1814, five days before the British navy reached Alexandria, the British army entered Washington and over the next several hours put to the torch the White House, the Capitol, the Treasury building, the Navy Yard, and other public and a few private buildings. This engraving depicting the British taking Washington appeared in a London publication.

❖

Above: This house at 711 Prince Street in this mid-twentieth century photograph was the home of William Fowle, who enlarged and restyled an earlier two-story flounder house that had been built before 1808. Fowle, a successful businessman from Massachusetts, was president of the Alexandria Canal Company. The house has been enlarged and renovated several times since Fowle's death.

COURTESY OF THE LIBRARY OF CONGRESS.

Below: The two large brick buildings in the center of this Civil War era photograph constituted the Jacob Hoffman sugar refinery complex on the west side of the 200 block of North Washington Street. The building partially visible to the far right is the Lloyd House at 220 North Washington Street..

COURTESY OF OFFICE OF HISTORIC ALEXANDRIA.

flour to the mills, bakeries, and docks of Alexandria and drovers who brought cattle to market. Located there were a blacksmith, coach maker, wheelwright, shoemaker, and tailor plus butchers (Hooff's Run was named for Lawrence Hooff, a butcher operating along its banks), tavern keepers, millers, and tanners.

Alexandria, D.C.'s first prosperity, and this latest resurgence, were led by a new merchant gentry similar to Carlyle, Dalton, and Ramsay, the earlier Scottish-connected gentry. This new group included the Daingerfield family from Spotsylvania County (shippers); the orphaned Smoot brothers from Maryland (coal, lumber, grocery importers, tanners); the Massachusetts Fowle family (flour exporters); Englishman James Green (furniture maker); the Swiss-Frenchman Anthony Charles Cazenove (importer, merchant); and the Quakers: Phineas Janney (commission merchant), Pennsylvanian William Hartshorne (dry goods merchant, wharf and warehouse owner), and Robert Hartshorne Miller (importer of glass, china, and other goods).

As an example of its prosperity, Alexandria could boast of Monsieur Generes, a French dancing master, who, dressed in a black dress coat, black breeches, black silk stockings, and pumps with gold buckles, taught his pupils on Prince Street, and held "practicing balls" bimonthly on King Street. Guy Atkinson rented well-lighted "Portrait and Miniature Painting Rooms" on 115 and 113 North Fairfax Street where itinerant artists painted

the portraits of Alexandria notables.

Then on the morning of January 18, 1827, another catastrophe hit the town when shortly before nine a.m. a fire broke out that rapidly destroyed the back buildings (kitchens, stables, outhouses) in the block formed by King, South Royal, Prince, and South Fairfax Streets. The fire also consumed 53 homes and warehouses on Fairfax, Union, Water (now Lee), and Prince Streets. Lasting five full hours, it did between $107,000 to $150,000 in damage.

The damage could have been worse if a performer from a circus that was in town had not, as the *Alexandria Gazette* reported, "mounted the highest and steepest roof in town…and sustaining himself by a shallow gutter within a few inches of the eaves" applied water for hours, saving the building and preventing the fire from spreading.

As Alexandria began again to recover, its economy received a boost from a new enterprise.

FRANKLIN & ARMFIELD

In 1808 importing slaves into the United States became illegal. Afterwards, anyone who wanted to purchase a slave legally had to purchase a slave already in the U.S.

In the area around Alexandria, growing labor-intensive tobacco had been largely replaced by growing less labor-intensive wheat. As a result, former tobacco planters had a surplus of slaves. At the same time, newly developing areas along the Mississippi River needed slaves to work labor-intensive cotton fields.

To take advantage of this imbalance, in 1828 the firm of Franklin & Armfield set up operations at 1315 Duke Street to deal in

African American slaves. With John Armfield in Alexandria buying and transporting slaves and Isaac Franklin in New Orleans and Natchez selling them, the firm catered to the needs of both regions. During the following almost nine years the firm became the largest slave dealer in the United States.

In Alexandria, Armfield kept his slaves on Duke Street behind high-walled yards, one for men and one for women, or chained in the basement of the main building or in outbuildings. Between September and May, sometimes as frequently as once a month, Armfield's men chained slaves together in groups called coffles and led them, frequently at night, down Duke Street to the waterfront to be shipped to New Orleans. There Franklin sold them to the highest bidder. Also, once a year, usually in late summer, Armfield sent a coffle of as many as 300 slaves walking the more than 900 miles to Franklin in Natchez.

One of Franklin and Armfield's coffles was described by an African American schooner captain named George Henry. He and a friend were walking down a street when they heard "such screaming and crying, we couldn't tell what it meant, so we kept on till we met about two hundred men and women chained together, two and two…. [T]he scene was enough to bring tears into any man's eyes if he had a heart."

The firm prospered—a researcher estimated its gross receipts for 1835 exceeded $24 million in 1970 dollars. Yet its success did not affect the inherent cruelty of selling women, men, and children nor did it make the slave sellers respectable. Historian Henry Wise pointed out a paradox: in the South "slave-owning was honorable but slave-dealing was not."

In 1836 Franklin and Armfield decided they had profited enough, began winding up their partnership, and soon Armfield moved elsewhere to assume a different occupation and identity.

FREE AFRICAN AMERICANS

Slaves were not the only African Americans in Alexandria. In 1830, over half of the black population of Alexandria was free, and many

free men and women had once been slaves. The Alfred Street Baptist Church, established in 1803, was the home of the first black congregation in Alexandria. In the early part of the 19th Century, the area around the church, between Duke and Wolfe Streets (later known as "The Bottoms" and "The Dip") became one of the town's first two free black neighborhoods. The east side of the 400 block of South Royal Street was the nucleus of another early neighborhood of homes rented by free blacks called "Hayti." The first Black Masonic Lodge in Virginia was established in Alexandria in 1845.

Many free African Americans had skilled occupations and were successful businessmen. Peter Logan was a ship carpenter, ran a boot and shoe blacking business, and became the Town Crier. Dominick Bearcroft operated a popular tavern at 315 Cameron Street across from Market Square (in a building now gone) famed for its crabs: "[H]e knew when they were fat and fresh—knew how to 'devil' them—to 'boil' them—how to prepare crab soup and crab pie!"

Freedom, however, was precarious. After the Nat Turner Rebellion in 1831, during which rebelling slaves killed more than 50 white people in southern Virginia, free blacks in Alexandria felt compelled to issue a notice stating their "abhorrence of the recent outrage" and asserting that they "would promptly give public information of any plot, design, or conspiracy" they learned about that might harm the community."

THE CANAL

By the mid-1820s, Baltimore and Richmond were beginning to take away Alexandria's valuable trade with the Shenandoah Valley grain

❖

A coffle of slaves marching in front of the Franklin and Armfield slave prison at 1315 Duke Street as depicted in an anti-slavery broadside printed in 1836 by the American Anti-Slavery Society of New York.

Left: A part of the Alexandria waterfront from which a small boat containing slaves is being rowed out to a ship that will take them to New Orleans to be sold. From an anti-slavery broadside printed in 1836 by the American Anti-Slavery Society of New York.

COURTESY OF THE ALEXANDRIA LIBRARY, SPECIAL COLLECTIONS.

Right: An image of the African American neighborhood Hayti, c. 1830-1860, based upon archaeological research.

COURTESY OF THE ALEXANDRIA ARCHAEOLOGY. SCRATCH BOARD IMAGE BY KAREN MURLEY.

fields. In a bid to regain that trade, Alexandrians subscribed $250,000 toward building the Chesapeake and Ohio Canal, which was to parallel the Potomac River west from Georgetown to the Valley. It would be the first of Alexandria's monetary pledges to the wrong business—canals. On the same day in 1828 that the canal held its groundbreaking ceremonies, the Baltimore and Ohio Railroad held its own groundbreaking in Baltimore. The race to the Shenandoah was on.

Alexandrians had to build another canal to connect to the C&O. In 1830, the Alexandria Canal Company was chartered by Congress, and on December 2, 1843, the *Pioneer*, at the speed of one and three quarters to two miles per hour, crossed the Potomac at Georgetown by a new aqueduct and wove seven miles through the old John Alexandria property to Washington and Montgomery Streets. It was the first canal boat to reach Alexandria, although locks were not completed to take the canal all the way to the river until 1850.

By then the new canal had cost over $1.2 million. The Alexandria town government had borrowed much of that amount, and over the following years it borrowed additional funds to maintain both the Alexandria and C&O canals. Meanwhile, the B&O Railroad reached Cumberland, Maryland, near the Shenandoah Valley, eight years before the C&O-Alexandria Canal did.

To help compensate for the loss of trade to Baltimore, Alexandrians expanded their fishing business. Operating out of a shambling collection of smelly shacks called Fishtown (which materialized from March through June along the waterfront between Oronoco and Princess Streets), free black women and slaves headed and gutted shad and herring brought in from

Potomac fisheries, washed them, and then salted and packed them in wooden casks for sale by fish brokers. In 1835, the Potomac River's total catch was 750,000,000 herring and 22,500,000 shad (demonstrating that fishing techniques had improved in the 200 years since Captain John Smith used his frying pan), much of which was processed by Alexandrians.

Despite this new trade, during most of the 1830s and 1840s, Alexandrians operated in what historian Thomas Duffy described as "generally declining prosperity." Still, in 1839, enlightened Alexandrians erected the Greek-Revival-Style Lyceum on Washington Street to provide space for literary and scientific lectures and for the Alexandria Library Company.

RETROCESSION

The great expectations Alexandrians held at the District of Columbia's beginning had been doomed from the start. Federal legislation creating the District provided (probably to gain Maryland's support) that federal buildings could be located only on the Maryland side of the Potomac. Thus, the federal complex developed on that side of the river, and Congress, although governing the entire District, concentrated on its side of the river and neglected the federally barren Alexandria side, except for taxing it.

Alexandrians, with Virginia's support, petitioned to return to Virginia, and on March 13, 1847, the town again became part of the Commonwealth. Alexandrians, more elated to leave the District than they were to join it, suspended business for a day, crowded the streets, and celebrated by firing salutes and staging a grand parade.

Along with concerns about taxes and neglect, some Alexandrians probably wanted to leave the District because they feared Congress would abolish slavery there and thus in

CHAPTER VI

WAR APPROACHES
1848-1861

THE TROUBLE I'VE SEEN

At 11 o'clock Saturday night, April 15, 1848, a 65-foot, two-masted schooner named the *Pearl* sailed quietly away from a secluded landing on the Washington waterfront loaded with 76 African American slaves. Her charterers were not slave traders, but abolitionists determined to publicize District of Columbia slavery, and she was bound for freedom.

Two of the slaves on board were Emily Edmondson, aged 13, and Mary Edmondson, aged 15, the cherished daughters of Paul Edmondson, a free black man, and his wife Amelia. Amelia was a slave, and thus under the applicable law, her children also were slaves. The sisters' owner had hired them out to prosperous families in Washington as house servants. Now, however, they were on board the *Pearl* sailing, they hoped, to freedom.

The *Pearl* made good time down the winding Potomac until arriving late Sunday evening at its mouth. There a storm was blowing from the north making it treacherous to sail up the Chesapeake to the ship's planned destination, Frenchtown, Maryland. The *Pearl*'s captain then made a risky decision, the schooner would anchor for the night until the storm blew away.

Earlier that Sunday morning back in Washington, word had spread quickly among the white population attending church services that many of their valuable slaves were missing.

Selling "fancy girls" in New Orleans.
COURTESY OF THE CARNEGIE MUSEUM OF ART,
PITTSBURGH. GIFT OF MRS. W. FITCH INGERSOLL.

Above: The Edmondson sisters. Mary is on the left and Emily on the right.
COURTESY OF WIKIPEDIA.

Below: Trade card from around 1857 showing Green & Brother Steam Furniture Works at the southeast corner of Prince and Fairfax Streets. By then James Green had turned over the works to his sons. The building now is a condominium.
COURTESY OF THE ALEXANDRIA LIBRARY, SPECIAL COLLECTIONS.

They soon discovered that the slaves had escaped down the Potomac, and a fast steamboat loaded with armed men set out in pursuit.

Early the following Monday morning, the steamboat found the *Pearl* still anchored in a cove near the Potomac's mouth. The frightened slaves and ship's crew offered no resistance. Soon they found themselves steaming wretchedly back to Washington.

There a few of their owners took them back, but most were sold. Emily and Mary Edmondson were sold to Joseph Bruin, slave trader of Alexandria (a model for slave owners in Harriet Beecher Stowe's *Uncle Tom's Cabin*), and transported to his holding pen at 1707 Duke Street, four blocks west on Duke from the former Franklin & Armfield facility.

Their parents, other free blacks, and area abolitionists immediately sought to raise money to buy the sisters' freedom, but Bruin had seen the sisters' good manners and pleasing appearance and decided they would bring a good price if sold in New Orleans as "fancy girls," attractive slaves bought for sexual purposes. He was asking the exceptional price of $2,250 for the two girls together.

This amount was too much for the local community to raise, and Bruin soon sent the sisters by boat to New Orleans. There they were exhibited on a balcony along the Esplanade and offered for sale in auction showrooms. The first time Emily was displayed in the showroom, her face was streaked with tears. Her angry seller said those tears lost a sale, promptly slapped her, and threatened worse if next time she did not smile.

Before either was sold, however, threat of a yellow fever epidemic in New Orleans and a promise by the sisters' sympathizers to purchase them caused Bruin to ship the sisters back to Alexandria. He gave their family and friends twenty-five days to raise the money. If they did not, the sisters would return to New Orleans.

The due date passed. Bruin had received no money.

A few days later, as historian Mary Kay Ricks describes in her book *Escape on the Pearl*, Emily watched out a small window in the slave quarters on Duke Street as in the yard overseers shackled slaves together in a coffle headed south to New Orleans. She and Mary waited for the order to join it.

She heard a banjo and fiddle begin playing to set the pace for the walk. She saw the prison gates slowly open, and she watched as the coffle walked out and away. Only then did she realize that it had left without them.

Their supporters had managed to raise a satisfactory down payment, and later with the support of churches and abolitionists in New York, they raised the entire amount to free the Edmondson sisters.

When the day came for the sisters finally to leave 1707 Duke Street, Bruin, in an odd gesture, placed a $5 gold piece in each girl's hand. To Emily and Mary, this gesture mattered little—they now were free.

After the extensive publicity their cause received, Congress began seriously to consider anti-slavery laws for the District of Columbia. Two years after the *Pearl* sailed, slave trading in the District was abolished. The complete abolition of slavery there had moved a step closer.

THE COMING OF STEAM AND PROSPERITY

The newly opened Alexandria Canal brought to Alexandria not only civic debt but also goods, especially grain, lumber, and flour and

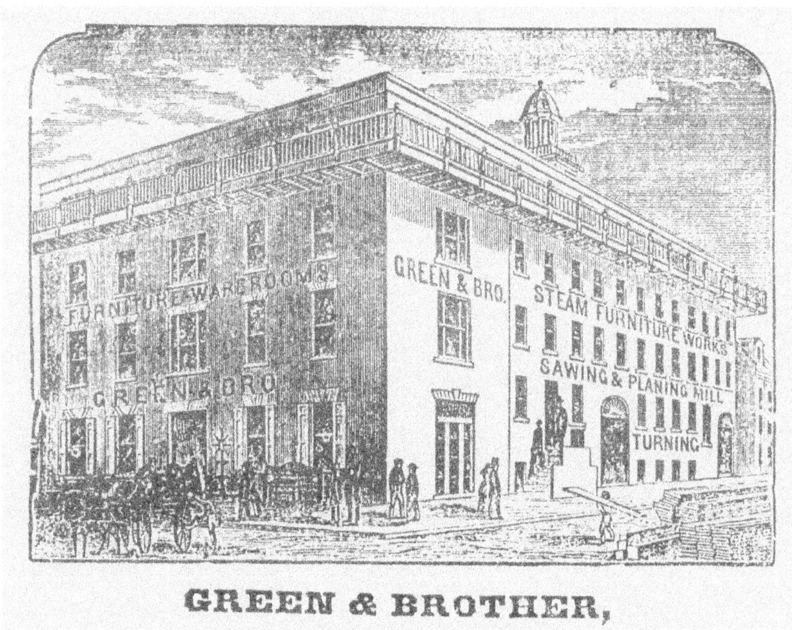

GREEN & BROTHER,
ESTABLISHED 1823.

later, from Western Maryland, coal. The first coal-carrying canal barges arrived in Alexandria from the west on October 17, 1850, and were met by a hundred-gun salute. By 1860 at least four coal yards operated at spots along the waterfront from First Street to Wolfe Street. In the late 1850s, Alexandria exported over 37,000 tons of coal a month. At times in the 1850s there was so much coal waiting at the city wharves that there were not enough ships to handle it. Rates for shipping coal dropped quickly, from about 20 cents per ton in 1817 to 1/4 cents per ton in 1850, with resulting reduction in the price of coal to consumers.

Before coal came to Alexandria, there had been little industrialization, primarily because the town lacked sites where water could be used to generate power. Manufacturing operations like early biscuit making and sugar refining involved little machinery and ropewalks required only manpower. Cheap coal, however, helped propel Alexandria's industrialization—coal powered steam engines, more flexible than water-powered mills, made large factories feasible. Alexandria began to change.

The change actually had begun earlier on a small scale. In 1831 at its factory on Union and Wolfe Streets, Thomas W. Smith & Company produced its first steam engine, a ten horsepower model used in its own factory. In 1836 the firm built a 15 horse-power engine that James Green installed in his new cabinet factory at the corner of Prince and Fairfax Streets to run power sawing and turning machines. Green's works grew to employ 140-150 people at its height and produce furniture said to be "as beautiful as the hand of man can produce."

Green's was only one of the new steam-powered factories that opened in Alexandria in the 1840s and 50s. In 1847, Henry Daingerfield, William Fowle, Robert Miller, and others incorporated the Mount Vernon Manufacturing Company, which constructed a cotton factory on Washington Street that manufactured brown cottons, blankets, heavy sheeting, and similar products. By 1850 it employed 150 men and women. Its machinery also was powered by a steam engine built by the Smith firm. Then in 1854, William H. and George Fowle and New York investors

The old Mount Vernon Cotton Factory building at 515 North Washington Street, c. 1930. It was used as a prison during the Civil War, a bottling house for the Robert Portner Brewery until Prohibition, and a spark plug factory from about 1918-1930. It now is occupied by the Masonry Lofts condominiums.

built at the foot of Duke Street a steam-driven flour plant called Pioneer Mill. At six stories high, it was one of the largest in the U.S. and used its 250 horsepower steam engine to make flour at the rate of 800 barrels a day.

The Smith steam engine firm added a partner, and as Smith and Perkins helped railroads come to Alexandria.

RAILROADS

On May 29, 1851, seven months after the first canal boat load of coal reached the Alexandria waterfront, the *Alexandria Gazette* reported that the first train loaded with flour "with an extraordinary scream of the steam whistle" rolled triumphantly down the tracks of the Orange and Alexandria Railroad on Union Street with an echoing shout of welcome from the gathered people of Alexandria. That first steam-powered locomotive, named the *Pioneer*, was built by Smith and Perkins. Finally Alexandria had a railroad.

Once Alexandrians became interested in railroads, they moved quickly. By 1861, four railroads had some connection with Alexandria—two to the west, one to the north, and one to the south.

In 1847 the first to be chartered was the Alexandria and Harper's Ferry Railroad. It was to stretch from Alexandria to Harper's Ferry and bring coal to Alexandria's docks. Not

Above: The building in the background of this Civil War era photograph is the Pioneer Mill. The photograph was taken from near Union Street looking northeast, and the Potomac River is just on the other side of the mill. The site now is occupied by Robinson Landing, a development of condominiums and townhouses.
COURTESY OF THE ALEXANDRIA LIBRARY, SPECIAL COLLECTIONS, VF-CIVIL WAR COLLECTION

Below: A locomotive built in the 1850s. This is the type of wood-burning train engine with a ballon-shaped smokestack that ran on the early Alexandria railroads.
COURTESY OF WIKIPEDIA.

Opposite: The ticket (ballot) for the Democratic Party's candidates for president and vice president in the 1860 election. This ballot was used in Richmond, Virginia, and the ballot used in Alexandria would have appeared much the same. It has the voter's name handwritten on the back and a small hole in its center where a voting official placed it on a spindle at the voting place.
COURTESY OF TED PULLIAM.

until 1859, however, did it, then renamed the Alexandria, Loudoun and Hampshire Railroad, place a train onto tracks. By 1861 its trains left the terminal near the intersection of Princess and Fairfax streets and proceeded out beside Four Mile Run only as far as Leesburg and transported to and from Leesburg primarily only passengers and mail.

The second western railroad was the most successful. By 1861 the Orange and Alexandria Railroad, under the capable leadership of George Smoot, had laid tracks from its terminal in Alexandria at Duke and Henry Streets southwest through Manassas Junction, Culpeper, and Orange to Lynchburg, where it connected to Richmond and Petersburg rail lines. Near Manassas, it connected with the Manassas Gap Railroad (also formed in part by Alexandrians), which linked Alexandria with the Shenandoah Valley by extending west from Manassas, roughly parallel to today's I-66, to Strasburg, then down the Valley, paralleling today's I-81, to Mount Jackson. In Alexandria itself, Orange and Alexandria tracks extended from its Duke Street terminal east through the Wilkes Street tunnel and then north along Union Street.

The Orange and Alexandria transported passengers and guano (fertilizer shipped to Alexandria from South America) to western Virginia and its nutrient-starved fields and then transported passengers and farm products back to ships docked along the Alexandria waterfront. Wheat was particularly in demand. In the 1850s, while tobacco exports were minimal (only four hogsheads in

1857) and flour exports increased but did not reach the heights of the 1820s, wheat exports soared. At the peak in 1857, Alexandria shipped 231,572 bushels of wheat.

The two lines commissioned freight and passenger cars built by each line's own facilities or by Smith and Perkins, John Summers, or T. S. Jamieson—all located in Alexandria.

The shortest of the four lines was the northern one, the Alexandria and Washington Railroad. It extended only from a turntable near the intersection of St. Asaph and Princess Streets to the Virginia end of the Long Bridge, which led across the Potomac to Washington (located roughly where the 14th Street Bridge is now). There the line stopped, and passengers had to disembark and board wagons to cross the bridge into Washington.

The last, southern line, actually did not reach Alexandria. It was the Richmond, Fredericksburg, and Potomac, which ran from Richmond to a terminus at Aquia Creek, on the Potomac just northeast of Fredericksburg. There passengers and freight boarded steamboats that regularly left to and arrived from Washington and Alexandria.

The steam engine was transforming Alexandria. In 1853 a writer for the *Rockingham County Register* wrote of the city: "the animation and occupation which enlivens her railroad depots, her wharves, and canal basin, as well as the bustle and hum of her streets, prove that this worthy daughter of the Old Dominion is in a fair way to rank, ere long, among the most prosperous cities of the land."

This new commercial vitality revived the Alexandria economy. Alexandria's population increased by 45 percent, from 8,734 in 1850 to 12,652 ten years later in 1860. Some of these new people were immigrants looking for jobs and business opportunities, like Irish workers and Jewish small businessmen from Germany. In 1860, Alexandria's orthodox Jews joined the Beth El Hebrew Congregation, established by reformed Jews the year before.

But other issues perhaps more emotional than industrial expansion occupied the minds of Alexandrians of all backgrounds as 1860 drew to a close.

UNION OR DISUNION?

On November 6, 1860, Republican Abraham Lincoln won the election for president with forty percent of the popular vote nationwide. In Alexandria, however, his percentage was much smaller. Alexandrians gave Constitutional Union candidate John Bell, who opposed secession, 911 votes; Southern Democrat John C. Breckinridge, who favored extension of slavery to the territories, 619; Northern Democrat Stephen A. Douglas, who favored allowing territories to vote whether to be slave or free, 138; and Abraham Lincoln 2. Many Alexandrians had Northern business connections and were unsympathetic to dissolving those ties, yet they also were leery of "Black Republicans" like Lincoln.

Out of a population of 12,652, 1,670 Alexandrians, about 13 percent, voted. This seems a small number in a heated election, but the only people permitted to vote in Virginia then were white males over the age of 21—women, slaves, and free blacks could not vote. Moreover, voting was not by secret ballot. On or before election day a voter got a ballot for the candidate he supported, brought it with him to the polls, signed it on the back, and handed it to a voting official.

One of the two Alexandrians who voted for Lincoln, Judge Andrew Wylie, later wrote that the election officials almost refused to allow his ballot to be cast and that later he was threatened by a mob. Citizens in Fairfax County, which had voted heavily for Breckenridge, seized a Lincoln voter and thoroughly blackened that "Black Republican's" face with printer's ink.

By February 13, 1861, seven states, led by South Carolina, had seceded from the Union, and Virginians were convening in Richmond to decide whether they also should secede. Alexandria's candidates for delegates were two lawyers, pro-Union George W. Brent and pro-secession David Funsten.

Brent beat Funsten by almost three to one, and statewide, pro-union convention delegates outnumbered secessionists two to one. At the convention, Brent made a well-reasoned speech favoring Virginia's staying in the Union. He rejected the argument that there existed "an irrepressible conflict of opposing and enduring forces" between northern and

Above: George W. Brent, Alexandria's pro-Union delegate to the Virginia convention on secession in 1861, in his Confederate officer's uniform.
COURTESY OF THE VALENTINE RICHMOND HISTORY CENTER.

Below: James Jackson, proprietor of the Marshall House hotel.
COURTESY OF THE ALEXANDRIA LIBRARY, SPECIAL COLLECTIONS, AMES WILLIAMS COLLECTION.

southern states and called on Virginia to unite with other "Border States" to arrange a settlement that would preserve the Union, which in its beginning, after all, "was pre-eminently a Virginia conception." On April 4, secession was voted down 45-88, with Brent voting against it.

However, after April 12, views changed. On that date, Southern troops fired on the United States army at Fort Sumter in South Carolina, and three days later, President Lincoln called on the states to furnish 75,000 men to confront the seceded states. This was too much for Virginia and Alexandria.

On April 17, the Virginia convention voted 88 to 55 to secede. (George Brent voted against secession but later wore the Confederate uniform and served with distinction.) The same day, an enthusiastic crowd in Alexandria watched James Jackson, a tall, tempestuous man (his biographer wrote that he indulged freely "the rude bent of his inclinations"), raise a huge Confederate flag atop the roof of the Marshall House hotel at the corner of King and Pitt Streets that Jackson recently had rented and begun operating.

On April 19, Edgar Snowden, editor of the *Alexandria Gazette*, who had strongly supported the Union earlier (and whose ancestor was killed in Braddock's defeat), castigated "the madmen at the Federal Capital" in an editorial and proclaimed that now "[Virginia's] sons will rally to her defense, without distinction of party."

On the same day as Snowden's editorial, Colonel Robert E. Lee was said to have been in Alexandria and read in the *Gazette* that Virginia was to secede. When he stopped by the Stabler-Leadbeater Apothecary to pay a bill, he commented to the druggist, "I must say that I am one of those dull creatures that cannot see the good of secession."

The next day, however, he wrote a formal letter resigning his commission in the United States Army. The following day was Sunday, and as Lee was leaving Christ Church, he was met on the grounds by men from Richmond who indicated Virginia needed his services. He soon became the commander of Virginia's forces.

Before secession was official, a statewide vote was taken on May 23 to ratify the convention's decision. Alexandrians voted for secession 958 to 48.

In the *Gazette's* edition the next day, May 24, one column over from the report of the secession tally, the first paragraph under the heading "Washington Items" began: "The fact that five or six regiments—from New Jersey, Michigan, the New York Twelfth, and Ellsworth's Pet Lambs—and perhaps others, were ordered to be ready to march at five a.m. this morning, created a great sensation throughout Washington…. [T]he nature of service on which it was proposed to send them is not yet known to the public."

Chapter VII
Civil War
1861-1865

THE FIRST DAY

In the darkness at 2:00 a.m. May 24, 1861, Union soldiers began crossing into Virginia over the Long Bridge (located approximately where the 14th Street Bridge is now). Among them was the First Michigan Infantry Regiment under Colonel Orlando B. Willcox. Its mission was to occupy Alexandria.

Also that pre-dawn morning, the Eleventh New York Volunteer Infantry Regiment, composed of members of the New York City Fire Department and commanded by 24-year-old Colonel Elmer Ellsworth, a personal friend of President Lincoln, boarded steamboats at the mouth of the Anacostia River and headed for Alexandria. The Eleventh was a regiment of Zouaves, distinguished by their uniforms of baggy gray pants and gray, waist-length jackets (both trimmed in red) topped by red forage hats.

In Alexandria, at 5:30 a.m. a Union navy officer from the steamer *Pawnee*, which was stationed outside the Alexandria harbor, came ashore and found Colonel George H. Terrett, commander of the southern troops in Alexandria. The officer informed Terrett that an "overwhelming force" was about to enter the city and that he had until 9:00 a.m. to evacuate or surrender.

Colonel Terrett's command included five Alexandria militia infantry companies: the Alexandria Riflemen, Mount Vernon Guards, Old Dominion Rifles, Emmet Guards, and O'Connell Guards (the latter two companies composed primarily of Irish-Americans).

Ten days earlier, Terrett had received from General Robert E. Lee, commander of the Virginia forces, a letter indicating Lee did not believe it possible for Terrett "to resist successfully an attempt to

Above: The Union locomotive Lion *on the east side of the U.S.M.R.R. roundhouse at the Orange and Alexandria Railroad yard near the intersection of Duke and South Henry Streets. The railroad administrative offices are on the left, and a discarded locomotive cab and cowcatcher on the right foreground.*

COURTESY OF THE LIBRARY OF CONGRESS.

Below: Colonel Elmer E. Ellsworth, commander of the Eleventh New York Infantry Regiment, the "New York Fire Zouaves."

COURTESY OF WIKIMEDIA COMMONS.

occupy Alexandria." With that in mind, Colonel Terrett ordered the Alexandria militia to assemble as quickly as possible at the intersection of Washington and Prince Streets.

As Terrett's troops were assembling, and before the 9:00 a.m. deadline, Ellsworth's Zouaves landed at the dock at the foot of Cameron Street and marched quickly up the street to the intersection of Cameron and Fairfax. There Ellsworth detailed a squad of Sergeant Brownell and six to eight men to follow him to James Jackson's Marshall House hotel on King Street where Jackson's Confederate flag flew from the roof. While still in Washington, reportedly Ellsworth had seen the flag and promised Mrs. Lincoln to take it down.

On the way they passed Joseph Padgett, Alexandria's night watchman, who followed them into the Marshall House and upstairs until he reached the second floor. Down the second floor hall, Padgett saw Jackson emerge from his room wearing his nightshirt. Jackson sleepily asked Padgett what all the noise was about. Padgett responded that the Yankees were on the roof hauling down his flag.

Jackson quickly returned to his room where his wife was asleep, grabbed a double barrel shotgun, and ran with it up the stairs. Looking up, he saw descending the stairs a Zouave private followed by a Union officer carrying his flag. Quickly Jacson aimed his shotgun at the private and pulled the trigger. As he did so, however, the private used his musket to knock Jackson's gun upward so that its blast struck Ellsworth on the steps above and killed him. The private then lowered his musket and killed Jackson.

Each side, North and South, now had its first martyr.

At Washington and Prince Streets, the Alexandria militia had formed up. By then Col. Terrett knew that the *Pawnee* had its twenty-four-pound guns trained on the city, the Zouaves had landed, and Willcox's Union troops were advancing into town. He ordered his men immediately to march out Duke Street.

Isabel Emerson, a lively, attractive twenty-year-old Alexandrian, looked out a window in her house on Duke Street just in time to see "our southern boys rushing by with their knapsacks on their backs and their bayonets glistening in the bright early sunshine." Just outside town, they boarded railroad cars on the Orange and Alexandria line that took them to Manassas Junction and the Battle of First Manassas.

By the end of the day, Col. Willcox's Michigan soldiers and the New York Zouaves had taken control of the city and began to cover its surrounding fields with horses, wagons, and soldiers. Willcox proclaimed martial law, which required Alexandrians to be indoors by 9:00 p.m. and prohibited them from buying alcoholic beverages. Soon enforced from the Provost Marshall's Office on King Street between St. Asaph and Pitt Streets, it also required passes, as historian William B. Hurd recorded, "to enter or leave the city, to visit the camps, or to be on the streets after curfew." In order to secure a pass, hold office, engage in business, or even fish in the Potomac, an Alexandrian must swear an oath of allegiance to the United States.

Within a few weeks, a fort named after Colonel Ellsworth was constructed on Shuter's Hill. Its main mission was to guard the city from a possible Confederate advance down Little River Turnpike and King Street, but two of its cannons faced, not west toward the Confederate soldiers, but east toward Alexandria and its citizens. For Alexandrians, the Civil War truly had begun.

THE UNION ARMY SETTLES IN

After the chaotic battle of First Manassas, July 21, 1861, General George B. McClellan assumed command of the Union Army in the vicinity of Washington and ordered troops into Alexandria in force to make it a Union supply and transportation base.

For the previous 112 years, the people of Alexandria had governed themselves; conducted their own businesses from their own offices, warehouses, and wharves; and moved about as they pleased. Now, and for the next four years, they found themselves in an occupied city, their lives controlled by the Union Army. That army had minimal interest in their welfare; its interest was in defeating the South.

The United States Commissary of Subsistence Department, with its Alexandria headquarters at the Old Dominion Bank Building (corner of Prince and Lee Streets, now the Athenaeum), was in charge of providing food for all Union soldiers. The Quartermasters Department, from its Alexandria headquarters at the Alexandria, Loudoun and Hampshire railroad depot on Fairfax Street, supplied the army with everything else except ordnance, such things as horses, mules, wagons, pants, tents, knapsacks, flags, shovels, bandages, blankets, and bugles. Quartermasters were responsible also for transporting all Union men, food, and supplies, whether by wagon, ship, or railroad.

Before the end of the war, the two departments had taken over the waterfront. They also operated in Alexandria at least one large bakery, a slaughter house near Jones Point, a mill, cattle yard, and horse corral, plus supply depots and facilities scattered throughout the city.

In March and April 1862, the Alexandria Quartermaster Department helped transport General McClellan's army and supplies (a total of approximately 121,000 men, 16,000 animals, 1,150 wagons, 44 artillery batteries, plus baggage, ammunition, and other supplies) to the peninsula between the James and York rivers without serious incident. In Alexandria a British journalist observed "a schooner laden to the water-line with locomotive engines…a brig shipping artillery horses by a steam derrick, that lifted them bodily from the shore and deposited them in the hold of the vessel. Steamers…black with clusters of rollicking [soldiers]." During part of that time, McClellan himself established his headquarters near the Virginia Theological Seminary.

Alexandria's excellent railroad connections south and west into Virginia were quickly seized by the Union army. In order to ease the movement of troops and supplies, the Union government soon constructed a line (supervised by 25-year-old Andrew Carnegie, headquartered in Alexandria) from Washington across the Long Bridge to connect with the railroads in Alexandria, all of which soon were united into one continuous railroad called the U.S. Military Rail Road. Its headquarters in Alexandria was at the Orange and Alexandria depot on Duke Street (whose roundhouse and general facilities the U.S.M.R.R. gradually improved over the course of the war).

As the war progressed, wounded from First Manassas, the Peninsula, Second Manassas, Fredericksburg, and other battles near and far poured into Alexandria by wagon, ship, or rail car. To receive and treat them, the Union army constructed hospitals and commandeered over twenty of Alexandria's large buildings, including private residences, and turned them into hospitals. Before the end of the war these hospital conversions included the Lyceum, Virginia Theological Seminary, St. Paul's Church, Methodist Episcopal Church, Lee-Fendall House, Baptist Church, Washington Street United Methodist Church, homes on Wolfe and Prince Streets, and the largest hospital in town, James Green's Mansion House Hotel on Fairfax Street. As one resident said, "The whole air was infected by hospitals." For those soldiers who died in Alexandria, the army also established the Alexandria National Cemetery, one of the first official U.S. Civil War cemeteries.

The Union army soon realized that Fort Ellsworth by itself was insufficient to protect Alexandria's valuable supply and transportation facilities. From 1861 to 1863, it built near Alexandria Forts Ward (which has been preserved and restored on West Braddock Road), Worth, Williams, Lyon, and Blenker, plus connecting rifle trenches, batteries, and log blockhouses. The army also added a battery of cannons, Battery Rodgers, to protect the waterfront.

One other Union organization set up headquarters in Alexandria. The summer of 1863, the "Restored Government of Virginia," Francis H. Pierpont Governor, established its capital in the city. The Restored Government governed only the parts of Virginia under Union control, not including the westernmost counties of Virginia that had become the new state of West Virginia.

❖

Above: Private Andrew F. Skidmore of the Mount Vernon Guards, age thirty-one. Before the war, Skidmore had been a carpenter and laborer living in Alexandria. In May 1862 he was in a Confederate trench at Yorktown when a sniper's bullet went through the neck of a soldier beside him and into his stomach, killing him.

Below: The Virginia Theological Seminary in the Civil War era. During the war, it was used as a Union hospital.

❖

Above: A rosette made by the Knights of the Golden Circle. The group's initials are visible in the rosette's center.
COURTESY OF THE ALEXANDRIA LIBRARY, SPECIAL COLLECTIONS.

Below: A scene at a railroad station in Alexandria in early 1862. Soldiers of a brigade of New York Volunteers wait for transportation to their camp at Upton Hills, Virginia, wearing some of the different styles of uniforms worn by Union soldiers in Alexandria during the war.
COURTESY OF THE LIBRARY OF CONGRESS. DRAWING BY ARTHUR LUMLEY.

UNION SOLDIERS

On Shuter's Hill and at various places around Alexandria, encampments of Union soldiers appeared. One witness described "grain fields that so short a time ago were looking so beautiful and flourishing, now covered over with tents, and trampled over with horses, and wagons, and soldiers and every thing pertaining to an army." In Alexandria itself one Alexandrian observed, "Many of the invaders have found quarters in the various untenanted houses in the city [those of Alexandrian's who had fled]...."

During the war soldiers from Michigan, Connecticut, Pennsylvania, New York, and most northern states camped around Alexandria, some to stay only a short time before moving on and some to serve in Alexandria guarding supplies, railroad yards, the waterfront, and headquarters buildings, manning forts, drilling, and enforcing curfews.

Like many garrison towns, Alexandria had its rough side. People eager to sell liquor to soldiers were everywhere, and some seventy brothels flourished with names such as "The Hole in the Wall" on Prince Street near Pitt and "The First Rhode Island Battery" at 33 Henry Street.

General John P. Slough became the military governor of Alexandria on August 25, 1862. (Alexandria maintained its own mayor and municipal government, controlled by Union sympathizers led by Lewis McKenzie, but it had comparatively little power.) Upon assuming power, he found "a reign of terror.... The streets were crowded with intoxicated soldiery.... The sidewalks and docks were covered with drunken men, women and children." Slough, "an eccentric and bellicose man," as historian William Francis Smith wrote, managed to quiet the mob.

RESISTANCE

Many residents, particularly fighting-age men but also women and children, left town before the Union soldiers arrived. One witness described the scene near the Orange and Alexandria Railroad depot in early May: "Such a dense crowd thronged the streets, carriages filled with people, wagons, carts, drays, wheelbarrows all packed mountain high with baggage of every sort, men, women, and children streaming along to the [railway] cars, most of the women crying...all looking as forlorn and wretched as if going to execution."

Many of those who remained were women passionately attached to the Confederate cause—their husbands, sons, brothers, and special friends were suffering and dying to oppose the Union occupiers—and they too wanted to resist them.

Their resistance took different forms. When Union soldiers hung a Union flag over the front door of Isabel Emerson's home, her stepmother, an ardent Secessionist, insisted that the family use only the back door. A group of girls aged ten to twenty formed a secret club they called the Knights of the Golden Circle. Its members swore to aid the Confederate government, not to help the Union, and never to marry anyone who helped the North or opposed the South. They crocheted items, such as rosettes, to sell to Union officers' wives and happily smuggled south the funds they received. Rougher women, according to an English journalist, "used to take pleasure in insulting the private soldiers with epithets which will not bear repetition."

Some remaining men also resisted. One Sunday during the litany at St. Paul's Episcopal Church, the Rev. Kensey J. Stewart omitted the prayer for the President of the United States. When a Union officer requested him to say the prayer, Rev. Stewart ignored him and continued the service. The irate officer quickly had Stewart arrested and marched out of the church. Stewart later was released, but the next day, Edgar Snowden's *The Local News* (Snowden's newspaper after his *Alexandria Gazette* was suspended because he refused to print the martial law proclamation) called the incident outrageous. The following night, soldiers set the paper's office on fire, destroying the print shop and two adjacent buildings.

Both men and women helped provide the Confederacy with information. Confederate spy Frank Stringfellow, a frequent visitor to relatives in Alexandria before the war and a graduate of Episcopal High School, spent over six months in Alexandria early in the war posing as an assistant to a local dentist, a Confederate sympathizer. Stringfellow sent through Union lines to J. E. B. Stuart reports on Union troop movements obtained by poring over Northern newspapers. On a later assignment in Alexandria, he reportedly was saved from a pursuer by hiding under the voluminous hoopskirts of a friend of his mother.

Still, even Alexandria women who supported the South did show concern for suffering Union soldiers. At daybreak on July 22, 1861, as Union solders streamed into Alexandria after being routed in the Battle of First Manassas, young Isabel Emerson at her house on Duke Street was surprised to find: "all along the sidewalk the poor fellows were sitting or lying, worn out completely." Despite her family's strong Confederate sympathy: "We had great pots of coffee made, and bread, and we went out and served them ourselves. They seemed so grateful and refreshed."

UNION SERVICE

Just as many Alexandrians abhorred the presence of Union soldiers in their city, many Union soldiers had little desire to be there. Still, most did their duty, and some even enjoyed it. Private Lyons Wakeman wrote home from Alexandria to New York: "I have to go on guard every other day and drill the day that I am not on guard. I like to drill first rate." (Private Wakeman actually was Sarah Rosetta Wakeman, a twenty-year-old woman who had enlisted to help support her family.)

Sometimes they did more than just their duty. As the Second Manassas campaign began in August 1862, some thirty thousand troops of General McClellan's army arrived at the Alexandria docks from the ill-fated Peninsula venture. They and their supplies were needed immediately near Manassas Junction.

Brigadier General Herman Haupt, the dynamic, 45-year-old head of the U.S. Military Rail Road, took a rowboat out among the fleet of transport ships in the Alexandria harbor to find General McClellan and request help with the transfer. Haupt found him, but McClellan refused him assistance. Haupt still managed to transport most of the troops and supplies over the old Orange and Alexandria line to Manassas.

Haupt also greatly aided the Union cause before the Battle of Fredericksburg in December 1862 when the lack of a rail line between Alexandria and Fredericksburg severely hampered supplying the Union army. He conceived the idea of loading onto barges entire railroad cars filled with supplies, instead of just the loose supplies themselves; towing the barges down the Potomac to a landing near Fredericksburg; and then simply rolling off the cars to trains waiting to take supplies to the soldiers.

Nurses were Union supporters who came to Alexandria voluntarily to lend their needed services to the wounded. Early in the war, Dorothea Dix, superintendent of nurses, selected only women who were over thirty and "matronly." Poet Walt Whitman, who on his own visited the wounded in hospitals in Washington and Alexandria, wrote: "The presence of a good middle-aged or elderly woman, the magnetic touch of hands, the expressive features of the mother, the silent soothing of her presence, her words, her knowledge and privileges arrived at only through having had children, are precious and final qualifications." One nurse observed, however: "Society just now presents the unprecedented spectacle of many women trying to make believe that they are over thirty!"

Nurses worked long hours and provided a variety of services depending on their skills: changed soldiers' bandages, washed and dressed their wounds, brought them meals, wrote letters for them, and generally tried to raise their spirits. Several nurses left sobering records of their service in Alexandria, including Jane Woolsey from New York, who worked at the Virginia Theological Seminary hospital, and Englishwoman Anne Reading at Mansion House.

CONTRABANDS & FREEDMEN

Besides Union soldiers, there was another group of people who came to Alexandria in great numbers during the war—runaway slaves. At first they were primarily young men. Soon, however, young women and whole families came through Union lines to Alexandria searching for freedom.

❖

A portrait of Brigadier General Herman Haupt, commander of the United States Military Rail Road.

Above: Contraband and freedmen dock workers on the Alexandria waterfront.
COURTESY OF THE ALEXANDRIA LIBRARY, SPECIAL COLLECTIONS,. VF-WATERFRONT COLLECTION.

Below: Harriet Jacobs, author and former slave, who helped contrabands and freedmen in Alexandria during the Civil War.
COURTESY OF WIKIPEDIA.

Their presence at first created a legal problem for the Union. In 1861, the federal Fugitive Slave Act was still in force. It punished anyone who harbored a fugitive slave and thus deprived the slave's owner of what at that time was considered his property. The problem was solved using the legal concept of contraband, which allowed one side during a war to confiscate its enemy's property. Thus the Union declared fugitive slaves owned by a Southerner "contraband" and "confiscated" them.

Many contrabands were employed as stevedores, wood cutters, laundresses, cooks, teamsters, bakers, and particularly as workmen laying track, constructing bridges, and building stockades for the U.S. Military Rail Road Construction Corps. General Herman Haupt, commander of the U.S.M.R.R. wrote: "These Africans worked with enthusiasm, and each gang with a laudable emulation to excel others in the progress made in a given time…." In the summer of 1864 a company of contrabands and freemen was raised in Alexandria to serve in the Union army.

After the Emancipation Proclamation went into effect on January 1, 1863, the number of contrabands increased. (At the end of the war, an estimated seven thousand freedmen lived in Alexandria.) To house some of them, the army erected wood-frame barracks at the west end of Prince Street. Others lived in houses abandoned by Southern sympathizers. Still others squatted in crowded shelters built in any available space from pieces of tent, blankets, barrels, boards, or whatever else was at hand. Shanty towns sprang up with names like Petersburg, Richmond, Contraband Valley, and Grantville.

To help pay for the upkeep of these new arrivals, the Union army charged both contrabands and free blacks working in Washington and Alexandria $5 a month. Some "free people of Alexandria" who had been employed by the commissary department since the beginning of the war protested in a letter to the secretary of war that they had their own families to support and that the $5 a month to support contrabands was unfair. Apparently, however, their letter changed nothing.

Julia Wilbur, a Quaker teacher from New York, and Harriet Jacobs, a former slave from North Carolina, worked together tirelessly to provide clothing, food, shelter, and education for poor contrabands and freedmen, often fighting against "the rapacity & cruelty of Contractors, sutlers, disloyal citizens…" and unsympathetic Union administrators. (As an example, one hospital administrator advocated housing contraband orphans with people suffering from small pox.) Harriet Jacobs particularly was responsible for establishing the Jacobs School, a free school for African American children staffed and managed by African American teachers.

To take care of the medical needs of sick and wounded black soldiers of the United States Colored Troops, in February 1864, L'Ouverture Hospital began operating off Duke Street behind the former Franklin and Armfield slave pen. Earlier a hospital for contrabands had been established on Washington Street between Duke and Wolfe Streets.

For those soldiers and contrabands who did not survive, a cemetery was established on South Washington Street, although the soldiers later were moved to the Alexandria National Cemetery.

THE WAR ENDS

General Lee surrendered on April 9, 1865, to great celebration among the soldiers and Union sympathizers in Alexandria. Loyal Confederates, like Isabel Emerson, were both saddened and relieved. "Thank God the war is over," she wrote.

Then not a week later, Lincoln was shot and died. Alexandrians, even Confederate supporters, shared in the grief and outrage. As Isabel Emerson wrote, "Whoever committed the wicked deed should be dealt with unmercifully." A railroad car built in Alexandria, probably for the president's use, conveyed Lincoln's body home to Springfield, Illinois.

On May 23 and 24 the Union victory was celebrated with a two-day Grand Review in Washington of General Ulysses S. Grant's Army of the Potomac and General William T. Sherman's western army. The latter group of soldiers, who had marched through Tennessee, Georgia, South Carolina, North Carolina, and Virginia, fighting most of the way, camped in the hills and fields around Alexandria.

Then, after the Grand Review and after four long years of occupation, the Union army left.

CHAPTER VIII

RECONSTRUCTION & RECOVERY
1865-1925

Confederate soldiers gradually began returning home to Alexandria, some with an empty sleeve where an arm should have been, "many others wounded and scarred," as Isabel Emerson observed. Some came from far away, like Dr. William Gregory, who rode a "sorry old horse…all the way from Georgia." Some, such as Private Edgar Warfield of the 17th Virginia Infantry Regiment, into which the militia units that left Alexandria four years earlier had been incorporated, had fought from First Manassas to the surrender at Appomattox. Some never returned. All who returned found their home greatly changed.

The city's wharves and warehouses were empty of goods and ships. The railroads were in disarray—engines and rolling stock exhausted, ownership questioned, and connecting rails, bridges, and depots in much of Virginia damaged or destroyed.

Many city buildings, like the returning soldiers, were wounded and scarred. At the Methodist Episcopal Church on Washington Street, used as a Union hospital, "the pews in the basement, and main part of the church have all been destroyed, the altars pulled down and damaged, and the one in the main part of the church (a marble altar) has been broken beyond repair" according to a Union army report.

Moreover, there was little financing available to make repairs and help get businesses started again. Confederate money was worthless. The city banks had little money, and the city itself, its revenue base eroded and burdened by earlier canal and railroad debt, was broke. In March 1866, the *Alexandria Gazette* reported that when checks written by the city were presented to the First National Bank, "the teller politely hands them back to the presenter, with the remark that the city has no money deposited in that bank."

Another immense change was the presence in Alexandria of over 7,000 free African American men, women, and children. Alexandria's population in 1865 was nearly fifty percent black, as compared with twenty percent in 1860. After the Union army left, many African Americans stayed in neighborhoods that recently had sprung up in the city or moved onto land, such as Fort Ward, abandoned by the Union army. Many had recently been slaves and were unprepared for freedom.

Finally, most Alexandrians themselves were demoralized over their lost cause and lost sons, fathers, businesses, and homes.

Still, Alexandrians quickly realized they faced two major tasks: bringing new life to the city's economy and determining how white and black people in Alexandria would live.

❖

A view of part of the Virginia Shipbuilding Corporation yard located on Jones Point, c. 1919. The shipways are on the left where ships' hulls are being worked on. The small white building on the river's edge near the center of the photograph is Jones Point Lighthouse.

How whites and blacks would live in Alexandria depended on who controlled the city and the state, and that depended on whether African Americans and former Confederates would be allowed to vote.

The recalcitrance of Virginia and other southern states in granting African Americans the vote led Republicans in Congress, over vetoes by President Johnson, to enact Reconstruction laws in March 1867. These laws placed southern states under military government and required them, before being readmitted to the Union, to adopt new state constitutions and ratify the 14th amendment, which provided "equal protection of the laws" to all U.S. citizens, including African Americans. Importantly, the Reconstruction laws also enfranchised African Americans in southern states and disenfranchised southerners who had participated in the rebellion.

Alexandria held city elections on March 5, just after enactment of the first Reconstruction Act on March 2 that enfranchised African Americans, but before there had been time to register newly eligible voters. Still, the day before the election, 200 to 300 black and a number of white Unionists met at the Lyceum to demand that African Americans be allowed to vote in the election. At the election itself, conducted in "a very orderly manner," according to the *Alexandria Gazette*, 1,365 ballots were cast by black voters but not included in the final tally. Hugh Latham, candidate of the Conservatives (former Democrats), was re-elected mayor.

The following year, however, under the new Reconstruction laws then fully in effect, General John M. Schofield, commander of Virginia's military government, dismissed the old and appointed a new Alexandria government with Republican William N. Berkley as mayor.

In October 1867, Virginia's voter registration lists compiled under the military government included for the first time almost 106,000 male African Americans (just 14,000 fewer than white registrants) and excluded probably 20,000 former Confederates. Voters on those lists elected delegates to a convention to rewrite

Virginia's constitution and gave Radical Republicans control of the convention. Alexandria's representative to the convention was white Radical Republican John Hawxhurst.

While African Americans experienced "the emotional release of being free" and avidly pursued education and jobs, striving to take part in the universally hoped for economic recovery, former Confederates were greatly disturbed by blacks "casting votes when many whites could not, sitting beside them in legislative bodies, strolling the streets without stepping out of the way, bringing their own crops to market," as modern historians wrote in *Old Dominion, New Commonwealth*. White conservatives thus began planning to take back control.

The constitutional convention, under the close supervision of General Schofield, adopted a new Virginia constitution. Among other things, it provided all adult male African Americans the right to vote, Virginia's first public school system, and independent status for all cities whose population exceeded ten thousand (which included Alexandria).

Before the state-wide vote to ratify the new constitution, however, a delegation of conservative and moderate Virginians negotiated a deal with federal officials and President Grant to allow two of its key provisions to be voted on separately, one requiring state and local office holders to take an oath that they never supported the Confederacy and the other disenfranchising anyone who held civilian or military office under the Confederacy. In exchange the conservatives pledged support for the rest of the new constitution, including the African

Above: A railroad bridge over Cedar Run between Manassas Junction and Culpeper on the Orange and Alexandria line wrecked during the Civil War.

COURTESY OF THE LIBRARY OF CONGRESS

Below: "The First Vote." African American men in line waiting to cast their votes wearing clothes indicating their different occupations.

COURTESY OF THE LIBRARY OF CONGRESS. DRAWING BY ALFRED R. WAUD.

American franchise. On July 6, 1869, voters defeated the two anti-Confederate provisions and ratified the rest of the new constitution.

Held the same day was the crucial first election for state officials and legislators under the Reconstruction laws. Despite African Americans having the right to vote, a skillful combination of Conservatives and moderate Republicans won the governorship and controlled the state legislature, giving old Confederates once again control of Virginia. As a Lynchburg newspaper proclaimed: "Shout the glad tidings, Virginia is free! …Virginians will rule Virginia."

Still, twenty-seven of the new Virginia House of Delegates were African Americans, including Alexandria Delegate George Lewis Seaton, 47 years old, a landowner and builder who had been born free.

In its session later that year, the newly elected Virginia General Assembly ratified the 14th amendment to the U.S. Constitution. As a result, on January 26, 1870, President Grant signed legislation abolishing military rule and readmitting Virginia into the Union. Reconstruction in Virginia and Alexandria was over. Now conservatives within the commonwealth could proceed to obtain long-lasting control without the interference of a military ruler.

The first election in Alexandria under the new constitution was held in May 1870 and pitted the Conservative former mayor, Hugh Latham, against Republican Mayor William Berkley. Latham won by 67 of 2,877 votes cast. Reverend George Parker, pastor of the Third Baptist Church, became the first African American elected to the City Council.

Then in 1872 it was the Republican Berkley who won in another close election. In 1873, however, Latham won election again, making Berkley, up to now, Alexandria's last Republican mayor. In the 1873 election, John A. Seaton, brother of George Seaton, became Alexandria's first black alderman, but the Conservatives controlled the Council and Board of Aldermen and would continue to do so for years to come.

It took Conservatives a little longer on the state level. Control of the state went back and forth until in 1883, Conservatives, reorganized as Democrats, won final control of the Virginia government and ended two party rule in Virginia until well into the next century.

In 1902, another constitutional convention adopted another new constitution and put it into effect automatically, without submitting it to the public for ratification. As prerequisites for voting, it required paying a poll tax (Alexandria had adopted such a measure in 1877) and passing a literacy and comprehension test that required voters to explain constitutional provisions. This constitution's main purpose, as state senator Carter Glass stated, was to "cut from the existing electorate four-fifths of the Negro voters." Predictably, local elections boards controlled by the Democrats enforced these requirements harshly on prospective black voters.

Earlier, in 1896, the U.S. Supreme Court in *Plessy v. Ferguson* sanctioned "separate but equal" state legislation throughout the South. The Virginia legislature in 1900 passed its first segregation law, requiring separate railroad cars for blacks and whites. Eventually, Virginia and Alexandria separated the races for most public facilities: restaurants, movie theaters, swimming pools, libraries, and even drinking fountains.

The question of how blacks and whites would live together had been decided for many years to come.

❖

Above: Signs like this one appeared outside bus terminals and railroad stations in Alexandria and throughout the segregated South.
COURTESY OF THE LIBRARY OF CONGRESS

Below: The Alexandria Marine Railway & Ship Building Company at the foot of Franklin Street where the Ford's Landing townhouses are now. In 1880 the company operated three marine railways extending into the river.
COURTESY OF THE ALEXANDRIA LIBRARY, SPECIAL COLLECTIONS, WILLIAM F. SMITH COLLECTION.

THE NEW SOUTH

Alexandria's economy recovered very slowly. For the first decade after the war, "Alexandria simply withered," wrote historian G. Terry Sharrer. There were even attempts by some Alexandrians, principally Union loyalists and African Americans, to persuade Congress to re-annex Alexandria into the District of Columbia, attempts that were opposed by most Alexandrians and failed.

In the spirit of the "New South" movement developed in Atlanta and Richmond, Alexandrians sought recovery through industrial development. They sought both to increase production of existing manufacturers and to attract new, large manufacturing concerns (frequently financed by Northern capital) that produced goods for extensive markets.

Despite its overall debilitated condition at the end of the war, Alexandria's infrastructure still could support industrial development. Its waterfront wharves and warehouses, while roughly used, were intact. The central city was encircled by railroad tracks that ran along Union Street to serve the waterfront, ran west up Wilkes Street, north up Henry and soon Fayette Streets, and back southeast to the waterfront. From this rough circle, connecting lines ran south, west, and north into Washington and the rest of Virginia.

Money from Maine shipbuilders soon expanded the Alexandria Marine Railroad and Ship Building Company, which repaired and built wooden boats and ships on the waterfront at the foot of Franklin Street. Josiah H. D. Smoot and Smoot & Perry operated extensive lumber yards between King and Queen Street, cutting up wood to make moldings, shingles, and other building materials.

Yet these were comparatively small-scale industrial undertakings. The most important industries in Alexandria into the twentieth century were the large producers of fertilizer, leather, bottles, and beer.

The Charles Calvert Smoot family had operated a highly successful tannery in Alexandria since 1820. After the Civil War, their tannery operations were located at a corner of Wilkes and Washington Streets conveniently next to the railroad track. At the tannery fresh animal hides were soaked in solutions made from lime, tree bark, and dung, then let dry in large sheds to produce high quality leather. Smoot & Sons was the only Alexandria firm to exhibit its products at the World's Columbian Exposition in Chicago in 1893.

Fertilizer was manufactured by the Herbert Bryant Company, located at the foot of Duke Street, and the extensive Alexandria Fertilizer and Chemical Company located on the west side of North Union Street between Queen and Oronoco Streets and at the site of the old Robinson Terminal North. The latter company used crude phosphate from South Carolina and Florida, dried blood and raw animal bone from western states, potash from Germany, and nitrate of soda from Sicily to make the fertilizer. It also produced sulfuric acid using sulphur from the Isle of Sicily and pyrites from Virginia mines. By rail cars loaded beside its

plant and by ships docked at its wharves, the company sent products to New York, New Jersey, Pennsylvania, Maryland, West Virginia, the Carolinas, and Georgia.

The earliest glass bottling plant was the Virginia Glass Factory, started in 1893 by a group of Pennsylvania Germans, and located in the 1800 block of Duke Street. It was joined in the early 1900s by three other plants: the Old Dominion Glass Factory in the 800 and 900 blocks of North Fairfax Street, the Belle Pre glass factory on North Henry Street between Madison and Montgomery, and the Alexandria Glass factory at the northwest corner of North Henry and Montgomery Streets.

These factories melted glass ingredients in their furnaces 24 hours a day, except for July and August when it was too hot for their employees, black, white, male, female, and children, to work near them. A large percentage of the Virginia Glass Factory's production was beer bottles for the Robert Portner Brewing Company, and the Belle Pre manufactured unique milk bottles using its own patent. The four produced glass products such as green and sometimes amber beer, soda, and medicine bottles, preservative jars; olive jars, and flasks.

The most successful of all these manufacturing companies was the Robert Portner Brewing Company, started during the Civil War by Robert Portner, a German immigrant from New York in his late twenties, and others. Under Portner's sole ownership, it grew to become the largest beer producer in the South during the mid-1890s and the largest employer in Alexandria. At its brewery complex (with its nucleus on North St. Asaph Street between Pendleton and Wythe), the company produced 100,000 barrels (about 3.1 million gallons) a year by 1895. Its beer, called "Tivoli" (spelled backwards "I lov[e] it") and "Vienna Cabinet," was shipped in insulated railroad cars, painted a vibrant blue and packed with ice from the brewery's own ice plant, to North Carolina, South Carolina, Georgia, and the rest of Virginia.

Between 1899 and 1909, manufacturing in Alexandria increased by the largest percentage of any city in Virginia, producing $4,420,000 worth of goods in 1909.

Yet, after the Civil War, Alexandria never seriously challenged its neighboring rivals, Baltimore and Richmond. For example, in the thirty years between 1870 and 1900, Alexandria's population went from 13,570 to 14,528, an increase of only seven percent. In contrast, during the same period, Richmond's population increased by forty percent.

URBAN LIFE

Life for city residents gradually improved. In 1881 the first telephone was installed in the city, and electricity came to Alexandria in 1889. Alexandrians even witnessed an early flight of the new Wright Brothers airplane. In 1909, Orville Wright and an Army Signal Corps lieutenant flew a test flight from Fort Myer to Shuter's Hill and back, passing over Shuter's Hill about 60 to 100 feet above ground and at nearly 42 miles per hour.

While along Alexandria's borders fire from glass factories lit the night sky and strange smells from fertilizer and tanning operations penetrated city air, much of Alexandria's commercial life centered on King Street. Here shops sold hardware, shoes, jewelry,

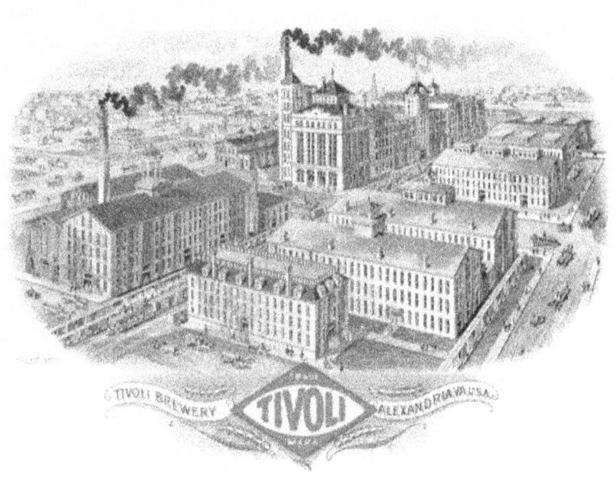

❖

Above: The Robert Portner Brewing Company complex in the late 1800s. A train runs through the middle of the complex on a branch line down St. Asaph Street.

Below: A group of men, boys, and a dog posing outside the premises of Terrence McGowan, Tailor, 300 block of King Street, in the 1890s.

❖

Above: Kate Waller Barret is seated on the right in this photograph of the Women's Party booth at the Panama Pacific International Exposition held in San Francisco in 1915.

COURTESY OF THE LIBRARY OF CONGRESS.

Below: The Confederate memorial statue (known as "Appomatox") at the intersection of Prince and Washington Streets with its back to the north, circa 1932. Standing in front of the statue is Edgar Warfield, former member of the Old Dominion Rifles, Company H, 17th Virginia Infantry, who first proposed erection of the memorial. He died in 1934 at the age of ninety-two

COURTESY OF THE ALEXANDRIA LIBRARY, SPECIAL COLLECTIONS, SOMMERVILLE COLLECTION. SCULPTED BY M. CASPER BUBERL.

furniture, bakery goods, and dry goods. Generally, businesses were on the ground floors with their owners living above. Shopping and strolling on King Street "and observing the shoppers and strollers" became "the main entertainment for young and old, men and women, black and white" wrote Marian Van Landingham.

From the foot of King and Prince Streets, ferries carried passengers to and from Washington and Maryland, excursion boats took sightseers to and from Mount Vernon, and steamboats carried passengers and freight to Norfolk, Baltimore, Philadelphia, Boston, and New York.

Alexandria women played an increasingly significant role in Alexandria and national life. When she was only 15, Mary Hunter and her mother opened a small grocery store on South Lee Street in 1871 that operated for 59 years, according to the *Alexandria Gazette*, without being "one cent in debt." Alexandria's Kate Waller Barrett was the co-founder of the international Florence Crittenton Mission that assisted unwed mothers. In 1919 she was appointed by President Wilson as an observer at the Paris Peace Conference that formalized the end of World War I.

Alexandria still was a proud southern town. On May 24, 1889, the city memorialized the service of its Confederate soldiers with a statue erected at the intersection of Washington and Prince Streets, the spot where the soldiers from Alexandria had assembled twenty-eight years earlier on the day the city was invaded by Union troops at the beginning of the Civil War.

Of grimmer note, the city, with the legal sanction of the Supreme Court and the Virginia constitution, began more formally to separate blacks and whites in public facilities and public life. In the 1890s, two lynchings of Black teenagers, Joseph McCoy, 19, and Benjamin Thomas, 16, took place in the city.

PROHIBITION & WORLD WAR I

In 1916, the city's large industries began to disappear. Prohibition became effective in Virginia that year, and Portner's Brewery closed its doors. Prohibition and numerous fires caused by continuous operation of their furnaces, also finished Alexandria's glass bottle factories, only one of which lasted into the 1920s.

When the United States entered World War I in April 1917, Alexandria, for a time, received new life. The federal government contracted with the Virginia Shipbuilding Corporation to produce 12 cargo vessels for $1,504,000 on a 47-acres site on Jones Point. On May 30, 1918, President Woodrow Wilson visited the plant and drove the first rivet in the first keel of the first ship, the *Gunston Hall*, built on one of the four shipways in the yard (parts of which still exist). The yard, whose motto was "More Tons—Less Huns," built nine ships, but in 1921, after the war's end, it filed for bankruptcy and went out of business shortly afterward.

A plant to produce torpedoes for the government was built on the waterfront at Cameron and King Streets at a cost of $1,216,655. No torpedoes were produced by the plant, however, until November 1920, two years after the war ended, and the plant ceased production in June 1923.

The fertilizer business and many small industrial concerns struggled and frequently overcame fires, floods, national financial panic, and other business challenges to survive well into the twentieth century, but by the mid-1920s, although unclear at the time, Alexandria's period of large industrialization was largely over. Alexandria would need to look elsewhere for its economic prosperity.

CHAPTER IX

NEW DIRECTION
1925-1945

WHICH WAY ALEXANDRIA?

On January 1, 1930, W. B. McGroarty, industrial agent for the Southern Railway and Alexandria booster, posed a question in the *Alexandria Gazette* about Alexandria's future. It was the beginning of a new decade, and he wondered what would be "the exact line of progress to which the city and community is destined. Will it be along the industrial lines for which it is so well adapted, or will it slip naturally, because the more easily, into the purely suburban class which its contiguity to a large and growing city [Washington] renders possible?" (By 1930, Washington's population was 486,869; Alexandria's, 24,764, only 5 percent of Washington's.)

Not surprisingly, McGroarty favored "an industrial Alexandria." This position was completely in tune with that of the Alexandria Chamber of Commerce, which for the past several years had been seeking new industries for the city. Using the slogan "Key To Dixie," referring to Alexandria's location as the northernmost southern city, the Chamber sought "manufacturing plants of all kinds." Its advertisements listed 13 particular types of industries sought, from shoe factories to iron foundries. Several small industries had located in Alexandria in the late 1920s, but McGroarty himself had written earlier that Alexandria "has not as yet secured any specific industries of the A-1 type."

In fact, Alexandria was slowly proceeding in the other, the suburban direction. On the same day McGroarty's article appeared in the *Gazette*, annexation of the largest territory thus far in

❖

An aerial view up King Street from the Potomac River to the new George Washington Masonic Memorial, c. the 1930s. The large gray building in the right foreground is the Torpedo Factory.

❖

Above: The town hall and firehouse of the town of Potomac built in 1926 and still standing on East Windsor Avenue.

COURTESY OF THE ALEXANDRIA LIBRARY, SPECIAL COLLECTIONS, SAMPSON COLLECTION.

Below: An aerial view of Potomac Yard looking south toward Old Town Alexandria and Great Hunting Creek, c. the 1920s.

COURTESY OF TED PULLIAM.

Alexandria's history became effective. By this annexation Alexandria acquired over 3.5 square miles and a population of 5,473, including the suburban town of Potomac and the great railway switching facility Potomac Yard. The annexed property, which was acquired from Arlington County, extended north along the Potomac River from the earlier northern Alexandria border at Second Street to Four Mile Run and west from the earlier western city border, located slightly west of today's Russell Road, to Quaker Lane.

This annexation was a strong indicator that Alexandria might look in a new direction for its economic future. By it Alexandria acquired not only the residents of Potomac (which had been formed in 1908 from two housing developments just north of the city, St. Elmo and Del Ray), but also land along both a streetcar line (running along what today is Commonwealth Avenue) and the Washington-Alexandria Turnpike (today's Highway 1) that provided commuter transportation links between Washington and Alexandria. To Alexandrians, incorporating new rate payers plus additional land with good transportation and fine growth prospects made sense.

Acquiring Potomac Yard also made sense. It was built by a combination of six railroad companies as a central spot to transfer freight between the northern and southern railroads—mainly manufactured goods coming south and agricultural goods going north. As the yard superintendent reported in the *Alexandria Gazette* in 1929, "practically every article manufactured, grown or mined passes through Potomac Yard." When it opened in 1906, it had 68 tracks and was designed to handle 2,200 railroad cars a day. It soon became the largest railroad freight transfer yard on the east coast. By 1929 it had 122 tracks and could handle 6,800 cars a day and employed 1,350 employees, many of whom lived in the new part of Alexandria.

Alexandria also was beginning to place more emphasis on tourism as a possible source of economic prosperity. Some of its first tourists came during the Civil War from Washington to see a real southern town, the place where Colonel Ellsworth had been shot, and Christ Church where George Washington had worshiped. Washington and colonial history became particularly good draws. According to historian William Seale, in the 1880s Alexandria and its colonial history began appearing in popular periodicals like *The Century Magazine*. The first part of the Washington, Alexandria & Mount Vernon electric railway completed in 1892 ran from Alexandria, not to Washington, but to Mount Vernon to carry visitors to Washington's home.

By 1930, new facilities had been completed or planned that were expected to bring additional tourists to Alexandria. In 1923, President Coolidge helped lay the cornerstone on Shuter's Hill for what would become the dramatic George Washington Masonic Memorial, a new and expanded home for mementos of George Washington's career. The tallest building in town was the six-story George Mason Hotel. Constructed in 1926 at the northeast corner of Washington and Prince Streets, it cost over $500,000 and contained 112 rooms. Then later in 1930, work commenced on the George Washington Memorial Parkway, which would pass through Alexandria along Washington Street on its way from Washington to Mount Vernon and would allow tourists to travel more easily to Alexandria.

THE DEPRESSION SLOWLY HITS HOME

Although the New York stock market crash had occurred in October of the old year, in 1930, Alexandria remained comparatively unaffected. Even at the beginning of 1931, the *Gazette* reported that unemployment had hit the city the previous year "but not seriously." At the beginning of 1932, the economic situation had worsened, but the paper still reported that Alexandria "probably has suffered less in comparison than most places" due primarily "to the fact that it is so close to the National Capital" and (in something of a turnaround for the *Gazette*) "that there are no large manufacturing concerns here."

On February 22, 1932, the local economy was bolstered by an estimated 100,000 people who attended a parade with thirty bands reviewed by President Hoover marking the bicentennial of George Washington's birth. That night a capacity crowd of over five hundred costumed guests attended a brilliant celebration of Washington's Birthnight Ball at Gadsby's Tavern. In May the Masonic Memorial was dedicated with another large parade and ceremony, again with President Hoover in attendance. Then in the fall, the Ford Motor Company opened at the foot of Franklin Street a plant for assembling and distributing cars that employed 225 persons. Despite these encouraging developments, for the

year, as historian Martha Feldkamp reported," tax collections were down, tourism was down, the [George Mason] hotel lost money, and the city's budget and salaries were cut."

The year 1933 opened ominously when the new Ford plant shut down temporarily in January because of a strikes at plants of Ford suppliers in Detroit. In March, however, Alexandria's four banks (including Burke & Herbert Bank, the only bank then that still exists now) survived the national banking crisis by honoring payroll withdrawals and even attracting new depositors.

Yet it was to be Alexandria's worst year of the Depression. By mid-December, 1,860 Alexandrians (15 percent of the workforce) had registered as unemployed, and on the last day of 1933, Potomac Yard laid off another 93 workers. Local charities ran short of funds. The value of new construction permits fell to less than fifty percent of that in 1932. Alexandria's economy stagnated.

Like America's other Main Streets, King Street suffered badly. "One day we took in $38 and were so thrilled we called relatives in Florida to tell them," recalled Bess Hayman, who, with her husband Ben, ran Hayman's family clothing store on King Street. On January 1, 1934, the *Gazette* thought it necessary to list for its readers the somewhat grim "ingredients necessary to a happy New Year." These were "courage," "determination," "faith," "hope," and "luck."

RECOVERY

In late 1933, new president Franklin Roosevelt's New Deal recovery and relief

❖

The Ford distribution plant in 1933. The large vacant area in front of the houses is the present Windmill Hill Park, also known as Lee Street Park..

Above: The Old Presbyterian Meeting House graveyard before being cleaned up by the American Legion. The intact table memorial in the foreground marks John Carlyle's grave. St. Mary's Catholic Church is on the far side of the graveyard.
COURTESY OF THE LIBRARY OF CONGRESS.

Below: The home of Dr. James Craik, Washington's friend and doctor from before the French and Indian War until Washington's death. The house, located at 210 Duke Street, is shown around 1928, before it was restored.
COURTESY OF THE ALEXANDRIA LIBRARY, SPECIAL COLLECTIONS, SOMMERVILLE COLLECTION.

programs began to affect Alexandria, and the *Gazette* reported that during 1934 "employment and considerable aid" were given Alexandria "by the Federal Government through its various agencies."

Also, as more people came to Washington to administer President Roosevelt's New Deal, its population overflowed to the quieter scene in Alexandria. The city's colonial history and older houses were particularly attractive. As the *Gazette* reported at the beginning of 1935: "Restoration of colonial houses continues bringing many new families to the city," much to the city's benefit.

Restoration of Alexandria, both by organizations and by individuals, had begun earlier. In one early restoration effort, the Second Presbyterian Church began in 1925 successfully restoring the Old Presbyterian Meeting House. In 1927 American Legionnaires helping to clean up the Meeting House grounds discovered a neglected tomb that was later dedicated as the Tomb of the Unknown Soldier of the American Revolution.

Meanwhile, in 1917, the owners of Gadsby's Tavern had sold much of the interior of its ballroom to the Metropolitan Museum of Art in New York. Nine years later, a travel book described the tavern as "a mere shell" with the lower floor being used as a junk shop and the upper floors "divided into cheap lodgings." American Legion Post #24 came to its rescue in 1929 and bought the tavern for $18,000. During the Great Depression, the Legion held onto the property and even managed some restoration work.

Possibly motivated by this new interest in Alexandria's history, an Alexandrian whose name indicates her own connection to the city's history, Sarah Carlyle Fairfax Herbert Hooff, instigated in 1929, with her husband Charles R. Hooff, the restoration of old houses in what would become known as Old Town, starting with the house at 121 Prince Street on Captain's Row. The same year, Gay Montague Moore bought, with the encouragement of Mrs. Hooff, the rundown brick house at 207 Prince Street and began its restoration.

This process proved attractive to people coming to Washington. As historian William Seale wrote: "Newcomers who liked old houses learned they could buy one in Alexandria for a very low price—sometimes under a thousand dollars—patch it up, wall in the back yard…and have a pleasant living situation."

At the end of 1935, the *Alexandria Gazette* reported: "Hundreds of new residents came to the city as soon as houses were available, and new homes were sold almost as rapidly as they were completed." At the beginning of 1937, a business census taken by the federal government "showed marked increase in the number of business enterprises here [in Alexandria] including a wide variety of stores." In 1939 the Torpedo Factory reopened, construction on National Airport began, and the *Gazette* reported that 1939 was "the most progressive in the history of the city," with the building total exceeding the previous year's record by more than two million dollars. It seems that for Alexandria, the Depression was largely over.

LIBRARY SIT-DOWN

A construction project creating jobs in 1937 was the building of Alexandria's first free library as a memorial to Kate Waller Barrett. It opened to the public on August 21. It did not, however, open to all the public—it was whites only. Exactly two years later, an effort was made to change that status in what was possibly the earliest sit-in demonstration in America for the cause of African American civil rights. On the morning of August 21, 1939, five young African American men between the ages of 19 and 22, William Evans, Edward Gaddis, Morris Murray, Clarence Strange, and Otto Tucker, came forward one after another to the desk librarian and requested a library card. When refused, instead of leaving, each got a book off a shelf, sat down at a table, and quietly began reading. The flustered librarian asked the young men to leave, but they stayed where they were.

The police were called, and when they arrived, they found outside the library a crowd of some three hundred people, including reporters and photographers. Inside the police reluctantly arrested the five young men without a struggle, escorted them outside without handcuffs, and later charged them with disorderly conduct.

Watching the proceedings from just inside the library door was fourteen-year-old Bobby Strange. As soon as the police arrived, he dashed off to inform the man who had planned the sit-in, Samuel Wilbert Tucker, a 26-year-old African American lawyer who had remained in his office at 901 Princess Street. Tucker had graduated from Howard University, read law in Alexandria, and only five years earlier had been admitted to the Virginia Bar at age twenty-one.

While an undergraduate student at Howard, Tucker had watched first-hand as Harvard-Law-School-educated, African American lawyer Charles Houston transformed the Howard law school from a sleepy backwater into a fully accredited, cutting edge intellectual institution. He also followed Houston's precedent-setting cases in persuading courts to require black students to be admitted to all white law schools in Maryland and Missouri.

Houston had not challenged directly the legality of the *Plessy v. Ferguson* doctrine of separate but equal but had shown instead that Maryland and Missouri had failed to provide African Americans with equal institutions. Tucker, however, wanted to attack separate but equal directly and outlaw it. His vehicle was the library challenge.

When the case came for trial, the city of Alexandria was represented by 31-year-old city attorney Armistead Boothe. Boothe was from a politically-connected Alexandria family and had been a Rhodes Scholar from the University of Virginia. In this case "he served as the reluctant agent of Jim Crow," as author Steve Ackerman wrote. He had been out of town the day the five young men had been charged and had no more interest in sending them to jail then they did of going. He requested repeated continuances of the case. In the meantime, Alexandria rushed to provide a separate library for African Americans.

In April 1940, the city provided African Americans a library (the Robert Robinson Library, now the Black History Museum) and over time quietly let the charges against the five young African Americans lapse.

The Robinson library had less money, fewer books, and shorter hours than the white library, and Tucker was disgusted with it. Still it was a beginning, and Alexandria's African American community used it. Before any further civil rights actions were taken, Alexandria and the rest of the United States were in World War II, and Samuel Tucker was in the army.

WORLD WAR II

On December 7, 1941, fifteen-year-old William Glasgow was hanging out at Timbermann's Drug Store on Washington

❖

Above: The five sit-down demonstrators being escorted out of the Alexandria library by the Alexandria police on August 21, 1939. In back from left to right: William Evans, Otto Tucker, Edward Gaddis, and Officer Jack Kelley. In front are (from left to right) Morris Murray and Clarence Strange.
COURTESY OF THE ALEXANDRIA LIBRARY, SPECIAL COLLECTIONS, VF-PEOPLE-GROUPS COLLECTION.

Below: Civil rights attorney Samuel W. Tucker.
COURTESY OF THE ALEXANDRIA BLACK HISTORY MUSEUM.

❖

Above: World War II draftees from the Alexandria area with bags packed posing on the front steps of the federal courthouse at 200 Washington Street.

COURTESY OF THE ALEXANDRIA LIBRARY, SPECIAL COLLECTIONS, MARY LYONS COLLECTION.

Below: With wartime food shortages creating many nutritional problems, home economist Ida Lansden explains to housewives from Chinquapin Village the necessity of preserving the vitamin content of available foods.

COURTESY OF THE LIBRARY OF CONGRESS. PHOTOGRAPH BY ANN ROSENER.

Street with some friends, when, as he remembered years later, another friend "burst out of the front door of his father's Palace Cleaners and yelled, 'They've bombed Pearl Harbor!'" One of Glasgow's young friends only response was: "Where's that?"

Several Alexandria families knew, however, exactly where Pearl Harbor was — they had a son, husband, or brother in service there. Learning whether they were safe was for some families a long wait. Not until a month later did the parents of Private Vannoy Herfurth learn that their son had been on his way to church in Honolulu when the attack came and was unharmed. He wrote home that he "saw the whole thing, but can't tell you exactly what went on."

Alexandrians were surprised when and where the war started, yet the fact that war came may not have been a surprise. Hints that it was approaching came in 1939 when the Torpedo Factory reopened and again in April 1941, when the first MkXIV type torpedo produced in the plant was tested in Maryland.

Soon, however, Alexandrians became familiar with air raid wardens, blackouts, meat shortages, tire quotas, rationing coupons, victory gardens, U.S.O. Clubs, scrap metal drives, draftees leaving home, and other indications on

the homefront that the country was at war. Families had on their back porches buckets of sand and five-gallon pails for water to put out fires from incendiary bombs. Antiaircraft guns stood at the corner of Henry and Oronoco Streets, on top of the Torpedo Factory, and several other places in town. Women in uniform walked Alexandria streets, to the approval of at least one young woman, who "admired them all so much because they were so well-groomed, with neat hair and polished fingernails."

Three weeks after Pearl Harbor, the city's morale was boosted when both President Franklin Roosevelt and Prime Minister Winston Churchill visited Christ Church to pray for "victory and peace," as the *Alexandria Gazette* reported.

Alexandria's first reported war casualty was Charles E. Craven of 113 North Columbus Street, second mate aboard a Standard Oil tanker torpedoed and sunk by a German submarine off the North Carolina coast on February 24, 1942, less than three months after Pearl Harbor. Notices would continue to come to Alexandria homes during the war as 101 Alexandria servicemen were killed. Many years later, Alexandrian Shirley Grimm Warthen remembered at the age of nine or ten learning of the death of a brother on Iwo Jima. Some of her small friends came to her door and handed her apple blossoms cut off a neighborhood tree and said, "Here, we're sorry."

Perhaps the biggest change the war brought about in Alexandria was in new housing. From 5,000 to 6,000 workers from as far away as Mississippi and Wyoming were employed in the Torpedo Factory. Chinquapin Village, housing 350 families, was constructed for them on the current site of Chinquapin Recreation Center and its athletic field. A trailer park was established in Del Ray, and at the urging of the federal government, the Metropolitan Life Insurance Company built Parkfairfax, a rental housing development consisting of 1,684 apartments that opened in 1943. (It still exists off Quaker Lane and I-395 as condominium apartments.)

Finally, on September 2, 1945, Japan formally surrendered, and the war ended. Soon, once again, Alexandrians returned home from war.

CHAPTER X

CHANGE AND PRESERVATION
1946-2010

No longer distracted by a war overseas, Alexandrians began to look around their hometown. Some saw things they thought should be changed; others liked things as they were. This basic disagreement, what to change and what to preserve, soon became Alexandria's central concern.

HISTORIC PRESERVATION

A postwar construction boom animated Alexandrians as it did people throughout the country. Property along Washington Street in particular became the subject of a number of rezoning requests from prospective developers. Yet the city's authority over construction there was circumscribed by the 1929 agreement between Alexandria and the federal government on the George Washington Memorial Parkway, which ran along Washington Street. The agreement provided that building activity along the Parkway would be "in keeping with the dignity, purpose and memorial character of said highway."

In early 1946 the National Parks and Planning Commission (NPPC) and the National Park Service, the federal government's monitors of the Parkway agreement, complained to the city council that it was allowing too much development along Washington Street, thus endangering the "memorial character" of the Parkway, and threatened court action. The NPPC even reported it was considering constructing an elevated roadway along the Alexandria waterfront as an alternative.

These threats gave the city council pause. By the end of June 1946, the city attorney, at the request of Councilman Paul L. Delaney, had drafted an ordinance, based on a similar ordinance in Charleston, South Carolina, that would establish an historic preservation district and create a Board of Architectural Review. The board would rule on the "appropriateness" of certain exterior architectural features of buildings to be erected, altered or restored within the historic district based on similar features of buildings in the immediate area. The board also would rule on the demolition of buildings built within the district in 1846 or earlier. A specific policy of the board was "preservation of the memorial character of the George Washington Memorial Parkway."

The Alexandria Chamber of Commerce, the Real Estate Board of Alexandria, Arlington, and Fairfax, and the Retail Merchants Association led opposition to the ordinance. They opposed the measure in part

A watercolor painting of restored houses at the northeast corner of Queen and St. Asaph Streets in the Old and Historic District. The narrow house in the middle is sometimes called a "spite house." Although possibly built to house a relative or servant, it also may have been built to spite a neighbor by blocking an alley leading to the back of the neighbor's home where he kept his stable and horses.

COURTESY OF ALEXANDRIA ARTIST TODD HEALY.

because it "infringes on the rights of the individual to use his property in a lawful manner" and would "prohibit the orderly development and progress of the City of Alexandria."

Alexandrians interested in historic preservation generally supported the ordinance. Earlier, the Alexandria Association (founded in 1932 as a private organization advocating historic preservation) had urged that buildings being remodeled or constructed along Washington Street be in harmony with Alexandria's eighteenth-century architecture, a concept that became the goal of Alexandria preservationists.

At the Council's stormy session on August 13, 1946, the ordinance passed, with the strong support of Councilmen Delaney and Thomas A. Hulfish, by a narrow vote of 4-3.

The Old and Historic Alexandria District established by the ordinance extended from the Potomac River west to Alfred Street and from Montgomery Street south to Great Hunting Creek. The board was composed of seven people, including two architects, a member of the City Planning Commission, and a licensed real estate broker.

Since 1946, the ordinance has been amended numerous times, and the board's decisions frequently have been controversial. Despite controversy and setbacks, the board has helped preserve what Peter Smith, the board's former principal staffer, called "one of the largest collections of eighteenth-century architecture in the United States."

SCHOOL DESEGREGATION

On May 17, 1954, the Supreme Court announced its decision in *Brown vs. Board of Education* declaring that separate schools for white and black children was unconstitutional. Virginia, however, in what became known as "massive resistance," fought school integration in the courts and in the legislature.

In September 1956, Virginia enacted laws requiring the governor to close a school that enrolled a single black student. This was no idle threat. Earlier the General Assembly had revoked Arlington County's right to an elective school board after the board outlined a desegregation plan for the 1956-1957 school year. Armistead L. Boothe, State Senator from Alexandria (who earlier had prosecuted the library sit-down demonstrators) had proposed giving a local school board the option to make its own decision concerning the pace of desegregation, but his proposal was defeated.

Whatever the Alexandria school board and its school superintendent T. C. Williams might have thought about integration, it had little choice but to followed the state lead, so that in the late summer of 1958, four years after *Brown v. Board of Education* was announced, no African American student attended a white school in Alexandria.

Alexandria then had sixteen white schools and three black schools with a total enrollment for the coming school year, 1958-1959, of approximately 11,500 students, 85 percent white and 15 percent black. By then the school board had completed much needed improvements to two of the black schools: Lyles-Crouch Elementary School, which had just moved into a new building in April 1958, and Charles Houston Elementary School, located in a building constructed in 1919 to which an addition had recently been added. (The third African American school was the new Parker-Gray High School, which opened in 1950.)

On August 11, 1958, twelve black students attempted to register at all-white schools closer to their homes than the black schools they were expected to attend. All were turned down. They then sued in U.S. District Court to compel the Alexandria system to admit them to those all-white schools. One of the lawyers representing the students was Otto L. Tucker, Samuel Tucker's brother and one of the library sit-down demonstrators.

When school started that year, Superintendent Williams immediately fired Blois O. Hundley, a cafeteria worker at the Lyles-Crouch Elementary School and mother of two of the children. At the following school board meeting, Williams explained, according to the board's minutes, that it was incongruous to have a school employee "suing the organization in which she is working" and that the firing "had nothing to do with reprisal" or her race. Less than a month later, however, Superintendent Williams, with board approval, offered to reinstate Hundley.

In January 1959, Judge Albert V. Bryan, Sr., of the U.S. District Court in Alexandria ordered the board not to refuse the admission of African American students on the basis of race. (Only days earlier, the U.S. District Court in Norfolk and the Virginia Supreme Court both ruled the massive resistant legislation illegal.)

Still the Alexandria School Board refused the students' admission. This time its decision was based on six criteria that on their face were racially neutral. However, when Judge Bryan reviewed the board's action, keeping Superintendent Williams on the witness stand for most of a day, he ruled against the board and ordered that on February 10, nine of the students be admitted to white schools.

After the board's defeat, Marshall J. Beverley, a former Alexandria mayor and candidate for the Virginia Senate, praised the "gallant fight" of Superintendent Williams and attorneys "to try and stop integration of our good public schools." He stated, according to the *Alexandria Gazette*, that "the hearts and minds of the majority of our citizens are sick over the thought of Alexandria being integrated." Of his opponent in the State Senate race, Beverley said "The remark of Armistead Boothe that we should all stop the fight and unite sounds like we should give in to the NAACP…I know the citizens will be law abiding and accept the court order tomorrow, but feel they will express their feelings at the ballot box against those who have helped and encouraged integration." In the following primary, former mayor Beverley lost to Senator Boothe by almost two-to-one.

On February 10, Kathryn, Sandra, and Gerald Turner; Jessie Mae Jones; and Sarah A. Ragland, escorted by relatives, "walked up the long hill to the spanking new William Ramsay elementary school and into the school main entrance without event" the *Gazette* reported. James E. and Margaret I. Lomax entered Theodore Ficklin Elementary School also without trouble. These Alexandria students were the first African Americans in Virginia to attend formerly all-white elementary schools. At the same time, James Ragland and Patsy Ragland entered Francis Hammond High School without event.

However, this peaceful first day did not mean all would proceed smoothly toward full integration of Alexandria schools. Early black

students in all-white schools were excluded from dances and sports teams, spat upon, and the object of racial slurs. Yet African American Sarah Ragland, only eight years old and one of the very first to attend an all-white school in 1959, remembered years later that on Valentine's Day, "I got a valentine from every kid in the class. My name was spelled a hundred ways, but that didn't matter. The message was there."

Gradually, through the actions of well-meaning people of both races, integration progressed. In 1962, Ferdinand T. Day, an African American, was appointed to the Alexandria School Board, and in 1971 he became its chairman.

Also in 1971, the 11th and 12th grades of Alexandria's three separate high schools, black and white, were merged into one high school, T. C. Williams High School (opened six years earlier and named after the former superintendent but now renamed Alexandria City High School). At first, all did not go smoothly. When the new school year began, the *Alexandria Gazette* reported that "a band of white teenagers pelted school buses loaded with black students." Yet at the same time, the fully integrated T. C. Williams football team "was undergoing calisthenics a few feet away on the Hammond practice field."

Coached by black coach Herman Boone and white assistant coach Bill Yoast, the football

The nine children who in 1959 were the first African Americans to attend Alexandria's all white schools.
COURTESY OF THE ALEXANDRIA LIBRARY, SPECIAL COLLECTIONS.

The yearbook photo of the T. C. Williams Titans football team of 1971 that was the subject of the film Remember the Titans.

COURTESY OF WALTON H. OWEN II.

Opposite, top, left: Before urban renewal, the view along the south side of the 500 block of King Street looking east toward Pitt Street from the corner of St. Asaph's and King Streets. The second floor of the tall building on the far left once housed an opera house and later a bowling alley. In the early 1800s, the Rembrandt's Shoes store at the far right was the store and home of silversmith Adam Lynn, Jr.

COURTESY OF THE LIBRARY OF CONGRESS, HISTORIC AMERICAN BUILDINGS SURVEY.

Opposite, top, right: Archaeologists and volunteers investigated an old privy/well uncovered in the 500 block of King Street during the 1970s downtown urban renewal project. The buildings had been removed and excavation had begun for the Alexandria Courthouse and parking garage.

COURTESY OF ALEXANDRIA ARCHAEOLOGY.

Opposite, bottom: In the foreground is the Murray-Dick-Fawcett House at 517 Prince Street. The front part was built c. 1774 making it one of the oldest remaining buildings in Alexandria. The exposed wood is the house's original, old growth wood. In the background is the Alexandria Courthouse constructed on the south side of the 500 block of King Street as part of urban renewal.

PHOTOGRAPH BY TED PULLIAM.

team's previous head coach, the T. C. Williams football team became the undefeated Virginia AAA champions. Upon its return home from its victorious championship game, as the *Gazette* reported: "A roaring celebration at National Airport was marked by black and white mothers embracing in joy." The team's victories helped ease the integration of T.C. Williams High. (In 2000, the team and its coaches became the subject of the movie "Remember the Titans" starring Denzel Washington.)

Finally, on opening day in September 1973, all Alexandria schools were integrated.

URBAN RENEWAL

Only a year and a half after the first black children walked into all-white Alexandria schools, the city faced another issue about change almost as controversial—urban renewal.

On July 19, 1960, city officials made public a plan for reviving downtown Alexandria prepared by John J Beggs, a New York urban planner employed by the city. The plan hit Alexandria like a bomb—both in the widespread destruction of Alexandria it proposed and in Alexandrians' explosive reaction to it.

According to the *Alexandria Gazette*, the plan proposed to raze 20 entire blocks of downtown, an area extending from Washington Street east to Fairfax Street and from Oronoco south to Prince Street. The only buildings to be spared in this area were structures "of acknowledged historic and architectural value."

In their place would be built a mixture of structures: a high-rise apartment building, a large parking lot, commercial buildings, an auditorium, and "a great motor hotel." City Council had not endorsed the plan; yet V. Ward Boswell, local real estate agent and chairman of the Alexandria Redevelopment and Housing

Authority, the city agency that had hired Beggs, told a *Gazette* reporter: "This [plan] is a must."

Adverse reaction was immediate and intense. The Old Town Civic Association, the *Alexandria Gazette*, the Alexandria Association, and even the Alexandria School Board, as well as individual citizens, opposed the plan.

The week after its release, the Alexandria City Council met to consider the Beggs plan. The *Gazette* reported the meeting was expected to be attended by "the most riotous aggregation of indignant citizens since the War of 1812." At the meeting, speaker after speaker opposed the plan, and one Alexandrian named Beggs stood up in the back of the room to announce he wanted his friends and neighbors to know he was not the author of the plan and was no relation to him. At the end of the comment period, Mayor Leroy S. Bendheim moved that the plan be rejected, and his motion passed unanimously.

Yet, the need for revitalization of downtown was generally acknowledged. Many businesses in the downtown area badly needed repairs, and as one official stated: "There are vacant stores all along King Street." When a young couple who recently had bought a home in Yates Garden took a walk on King Street, the woman looked around and told her husband, "We've made a mistake."

The amount of taxes downtown businesses paid was an indication of their declining health. Tax records for the previous year indicated that 76 merchants in the area covered by the plan each paid less than $101 a year in taxes and that businesses there paid real estate taxes amounting to only 2.25 percent of total city receipts. "As shopping centers were built in outlying areas, many consumers preferred to stay away from downtown where parking was difficult and after dark the area was considered unsafe," wrote historian Patricia Ellen McClosky. Renovation might bring customers back downtown.

Many preservationists themselves were not against urban renewal entirely, but they wanted to be part of the planning process. When the City Council in August 1960 instructed the city planner to complete a new urban renewal plan, it also appointed a citizens' advisory committee to review it.

On June 18, 1963, the Council approved the Gadsby Commercial Urban Renewal Plan, named after Gadsby's Tavern, which was to be preserved. The plan was to be implemented in three phases: under Phase 1, two entire blocks, the one where Gadsby's was located (to be called Tavern Square) and the City Hall block (referred to as Market Square), would be developed; Phase II covered the south side of the 300, 400, and 500 blocks of King Street and the north side of the 500 block of King; and Phase III was to develop the 600 block of King Street.

Approval did not end the controversy over the development as it progressed, which included heated battles at the Board of Architectural Review and City Council over the preservation of individual buildings and the appearance of structures that would replace them. Still, Tavern Square and Market Square (Phase I) were completed in June 1967 and the last of Phase II was completed in 1981. Phase III was never implemented.

THE WATERFRONT

In the 1950s and 1960s, the waterfront was viewed as different from other parts of downtown, partly because for almost its entire length it was separated from downtown shops and homes by the old railroad that exited the Wilkes Street tunnel and ran along Union Street and partly because most of Alexandria's remaining industrial sites were located along the waterfront.

Those facilities, however, had gradually become disused and had deteriorated. Also, only a few ships a year docked along the waterfront at only a few places, such as the Robinson Terminal Warehouse Corporation's wharves at the foot of Oronoco Street (on old West's Point) and the foot of Duke Street (old Point Lumley) where they unloaded mainly newsprint from Canada and Scandinavia. Along the water were pockets of neglected lots and rotting wharves, such as the "Barge Wharf" lot at the foot of Wolfe Street containing, as described in the *Gazette*, "eight ramshackle structures consisting of shacks, barges on foundations, and outhouses and sheds" that had become "a gathering place for tramps, vagrants, alcoholics, and drunkards."

In the late 1960s, the old Alexandria Fertilizer and Chemical Factory property on the west side

of Union Street between Queen and Oronoco was developed into a complex of three-story homes known as the Brandt Townhouses. Possibly encouraged by this successful residential development, in December 1971, Watergate Improvements, Inc., filed plans with the city Planning Commission to construct a 650-unit condominium complex on the two block area on the waterfront bounded by Union, Oronoco, and Queen Streets (site of old Fishtown). The complex would consist of four 18-story buildings, each set upon 20-foot stilts and rising 178 feet in the air.

A number of Alexandria residents, including Ellen Pickering and Robert L. Montague III, opposed the project, arguing it would "tower over historic Old Town," and increase traffic, air pollution, water pollution, and noise. Supporters, such as the Alexandria Board of Trade, contended it would add about $600,000 to the city income, and as Councilman Wiley Mitchell said, "turn a neglected area of blight into a prime urban asset." In March 1972 the council unanimously approved the project after attaching 43 conditions worked out with Watergate Improvements.

Defeated by the city council, opponents of the development filed suit against the city and Watergate in Alexandria's circuit court in June 1972, contending that the city did not own the land on which the project would be built. The U.S. Department of the Interior agreed. It had long contended that the United

States owned that land, and in December 1973, the U.S. attorney general entered the courts with a suit to quiet title to 22 tracts of waterfront property from Daingerfield Island to Jones Point Park.

The suit's key issue concerned the location of the boundary between the District of Columbia and Virginia after the 1632 grant from King Charles I establishing the Virginia bank of the Potomac as Maryland's boundary, Virginia's ceding property to form the District of Columbia in 1791, the federal government's retrocession of property along the Potomac waterfront to Virginia in 1847, and subsequent federal and Virginia actions. Because of the complexity of this issue, for years to come individual property settlements entered into as part of the suit established frameworks for resolving waterfront development issues. As of 2010, seven tracts still were part of the court action. (The proposed Watergate site is now Founders Park.)

The old Torpedo Plant was one area along the waterfront not part of a suit. The city had purchased the property from the federal government in 1970, before suits were filed. In 1974, largely through the efforts of artist Marian Van Landingham, one of the four buildings of the complex became the Torpedo Factory Art Center. In 2010, it was home to 80-plus studios, six galleries, over 160 artists, the Art League School, print making classes, and the Alexandria Archaeology Museum.

THE CITY AS HISTORIC PRESERVATION CUSTODIAN

In 1965, in the midst of urban renewal, the Smithsonian Institution financed Richard Muzzrole to do "salvage archaeology," examining Alexandria's wells and privies uncovered by bulldozers and saving what artifacts he could. When the Smithsonian's program ended in June 1971, Muzzrole continued his excavations using his own money and funds provided by a group of Alexandrians until in 1973, prodded by citizens, the city created its first archaeology position. In 1975 the city established the Alexandria Archaeology Commission to provide formal citizen involvement in the archaeology program, the first such commission in the country, and in 1977 hired Pamela J. Cressey to be the city's head archaeologist. One of her principal duties became managing Alexandria's Archaeology Protection Code adopted in 1989.

The city gradually took over and began managing many of Alexandria's historic properties, such as Gadsby's Tavern, Fort Ward, and Freedom House Museum (the former Franklin-Armfield slave pen). To help preserve Alexandria's story, the city named a full-time historian, T. Michael Miller; started the Special Collections-Local History branch of the Alexandria library; and established the Archives and Records Center. In 1984 the city created a second historic district, the Parker-Gray District, which included an area from North Alfred Street west to North West Street and from Cameron Street north to First Street.

In addition, Carlyle House, the Athenaeum, and the Lee-Fendall House have been preserved by non-profit organizations, and Alexandria churches have preserved their historic places of worship. A number of other non-profit organizations have been established to promote historic preservation and education. Also individuals, such as Marianne (Polly) Hulfish, continued to restore Alexandria's historic old homes.

ANNEXATION AND NEW COMMUNITIES

In 1952, Alexandria annexed from Fairfax County the largest geographical area added in its history, an area bounded by Quaker Lane on the east, King Street-Route 7 on the north, a rambling curve from King Street to the Southern Railroad on the west, and roughly today's beltway on the south.

The annexation encompassed Landmark Mall, Cameron Station and Ben Brenman Park (site of the Union army's Camp California during the Civil War and a U.S. army

quartermaster depot during World War II), the Carlyle and Eisenhower Valley developments, and the Virginia Theological Seminary and Episcopal High School. Today part of the area is the location of vibrant Latino and Ethiopian communities. (In 2010, Alexandria school authorities reported that English, Spanish, and depending on the year, Amharic—the language of Ethiopia—or Arabic were the languages most spoken by T. C. Williams High School students and that 29 percent of its students were foreign born.)

With this annexation, the site of Alexandria's first rival, the 1740s village of Cameron, became part of the city, although Cameron itself long ago ceased to exist. The annexation also brought into the city the homesite of the Alexandria area's first known European inhabitant, seventeenth century's John Coggins.

NEW LEADERSHIP

Since Margaret Brent was the first European to own land in the future Alexandria, accomplished women have been associated with Alexandria. It was not until after World War II, however, that women began to take principal leadership roles in city government and represent the city on the state level.

In 1954, Irene Pancoast became Alexandria's first female judge when appointed to the Juvenile and Domestic Relations Court. In 1963, Marion Galland was elected the first Alexandria woman to serve in the Virginia House of Delegates. In 1973 Alexandrians elected Nora Lamborne and Beverly Beidler, the first women on the city council, later followed by long-term council member Del Pepper. Vola Lawson was appointed the first female city manager in 1985, and, in 1991, Patricia Ticer was elected the city's first woman mayor. In 1995, Ticer was elected the first woman from Alexandria to serve in the Virginia Senate.

Formerly the site of the largest slave trading company in the United States, in 2003 Alexandria elected African American William Euille as its mayor.

CONCLUSION

Alexandrians have faced numerous challenges—agricultural shifts, financial failures, industrial and technological changes, fires, and devastating wars—yet again and again adapted, recovered, survived, and even flourished. And as they adapted, they managed to preserve the historical structures, artifacts, and stories that made, and continue to make, Alexandria unique.

In its latest adaptation, Alexandria is no longer an industrial or international shipping city. Instead, according to the city's website, it has "a growing base of high-technology firms, management consulting companies, professional services, and trade and professional association headquarters," many of which value the city's proximity to Washington. In addition, its historical museums, Torpedo Factory Art Center, shops, restaurants, and historical atmosphere have made Alexandria a prime tourist destination. Perhaps most importantly, families who have their roots in the city and people from many parts of the United States and the world continue to find Alexandria a delightful place to live.

"Alexandria's history, of course, continues. It also continues to be discovered. In 20002, a cache of 4,000 of Robert E. Lee's family papers was found in two old steamer trunks stored for 84 years in a basement vault at Burke & Herbert Bank & Trust Company. In 2009, Alexandrians began rediscovering a community of former slaves who settled on the grounds of Fort Ward immediately after the Civil War. Between 2015 and 2018, archaeologists working on the Alexandria waterfront excavated the remains of hulls of four historic sailing ships. And, while digging at the site of the Contrabands and Freedmen's Cemetery early this century, archaeologists discovered a Clovis spear point broken and left behind at the future site of Alexandria by an Indian stone worker some thirteen thousand years ago."

Top, left: Virginia State Senator and former Alexandria Mayor Patricia S. Ticer.
COURTESY OF THE ALEXANDRIA LIBRARY, SPECIAL COLLECTIONS, NINA TISARA COLLECTION.

Below: Alexandria Mayor William D. Euille.
COURTESY OF MATTOX PHOTOGRAPHY.

BIBLIOGRAPHY

There are numerous sources for this book, and a footnoted version of the text will be available in the Special Collections/Local History Branch of the Alexandria Library. The principal sources are as follows:

Abbot, W. W., et al, eds. *The Papers of George Washington*. Charlottesville: The University Press of Virginia, 1983- .

Ackerman, Stephen J. "The Trials of S. W. Tucker." *Washington Post Magazine*, June 11, 2000.

Alexandria Gazette, 1784-2009, Microfilm, Special Collections/Local History, Alexandria Library.

Barber, James G. *Alexandria in the Civil War*. Lynchburg, Virginia: H.E. Howard, Inc., 1988.

Cressey, Pamela J. "The Alexandria, Virginia City-Site: Archaeology in an Afro-American Neighborhood, 1830-1910." Ph.D diss., The University of Iowa, 1985.

Feldkamp, Martha S. "A History of Alexandria, Virginia, in the Depression Years of 1930-1934." Master's thesis, The George Washington University, 1977.

Hambleton, Elizabeth and Marian Van Landingham, eds. *Alexandria: A Composite History*. Alexandria: The Alexandria Bicentennial Commission, 1975.

Heineman, Ronald L., John G. Kolp, Anthony S. Parent, Jr., and William G. Shade. *Old Dominion, New Commonwealth: A History of Virginia, 1607-2007*. Charlottesville: The University Press of Virginia, 2007.

Howard, Mark. "An Historical Study of the Desegregation of the Alexandria, Virginia, City Public Schools, 1954-1973." Ph.D. diss., The George Washington University, 1976.

Hurd, William B. *Alexandria, Virginia, 1861-1865*. Alexandria: Fort Ward Museum, 1970, 3rd ed., 1980.

Kundahl, George G. *Alexandria Goes to War: Beyond Robert E. Lee*. Knoxville: The University of Tennessee Press, 2004.

McCloskey, Patricia Ellen. "Urban Renewal and Historic Preservation: A Case Study of Alexandria, Virginia, 1945-1980." Master's thesis, The George Washington University, 1999.

Macoll, John D. and George J. Stansfield, eds. *Alexandria: A Towne in Transition, 1800-1900*. Alexandria: Alexandria Bicentennial Commission and Alexandria Historical Society, 1977.

McCardell, Lee. *Ill-Starred General: Braddock of the Coldstream Guards*. Pittsburgh: University of Pittsburgh Press, 1986.

Miller, T. Michael. "The Homefront: Wartime Alexandria, 1941-1945, Parts I and II." *The Fireside Sentinel*, vol. VII, nos. 1 and 2 (January/February 1993 and March/April 1993).

Miller, T. Michael, ed. *Pen Portraits of Alexandria, Virginia, 1739-1900*. Bowie, Maryland: Heritage Books, Inc., 1987.

Munson, James. *Colo. John Carlyle, Gent.: A True and Just Account of the Man and His House*. Northern Virginia: Northern Virginia Regional Park Authority, 1986.

Pippenger, Wesley E. *John Alexander: A Northern Neck Proprietor, His Family, Friends and Kin*. Baltimore: Gateway Press, Inc., 1990.

Rice, James D. *Nature & History in the Potomac Country: From Hunter-Gatherers to the Age of Jefferson*. Baltimore: The Johns Hopkins University Press, 2009.

Ricks, Mary Kay. *Escape on the Pearl: The Heroic Bid for Freedom on the Underground Railroad*. New York: HarperCollins Publishers, 2007.

Robbins, Allan W., ed. "Alexandria in the War of 1812." *Alexandria History*, vol. VI (1984).

Shomette, Donald G. *Maritime Alexandria: The Rise and Fall of an American Entrepot*. Westminster, Maryland: Heritage Books, 2005.

Sizemore, Bobby. "George Johnston: Forgotten Patriot." *Northern Virginia Heritage*, vol. 3 (1981).

Smith, J. Douglas. *Managing White Supremacy: Race, Politics, and Citizenship in Jim Crow Virginia*. Chapel Hill: The University of North Carolina Press, 2002.

Smith, Peter H. "The Beginning of Historic Preservation in Alexandria – Moving Toward the Creation of the Old and Historic District." *The Alexandria Chronicle*, vol. IV (winter 1996).

Smith, William Francis and T. Michael Miller. *A Seaport Saga: Portrait of Old Alexandria, Virginia*. Virginia Beach: The Downing Company Publishers, 1989, 3rd ed., 2001.

United States Navy Department. *Naval Documents of the American Revolution*. 8 vols. Washington, D.C.: U. S. Government Printing Office, 1964-1980.

United States War Department. *The War of the Rebellion: A Compilation of the Official Records of the Union and Confederate Armies*. 128 vols. Washington, D.C.: U.S. Government Printing Office, 1880-1901.

Wahll, Andrew J. *Braddock Road Chronicles 1755*. Bowie, Maryland: Heritage Books, 1999.

About the Author

TED PULLIAM

Ted Pulliam's articles have appeared in Legal Times, *WWII History* magazine, *American History* magazine, the *Washington Post*, and other publications. He is the author of *True Tales of Old Alexandria*, a selection of stories from the history of Alexandria and surrounding area from 1623 to 2023 and editor (under Edward H. Pulliam) of *Here's a Letter from Thy Dear Son*, an annotated collection of more than 200 letters written by a Georgia farming family before, during, and after the Civil War.

A current member of the Alexandria Archaeological Commission and the Alexandria African American Heritage Trail Commission, he also is a past member of the board of the Alexandria Historical Society and the Alexandria Waterfront Commission. He has received the award given annually by the Historical Society for making "especially noteworthy contributions to the preservation of the historic, cultural, and artistic heritage of Alexandria."

He is a graduate of Davidson College and Columbia University Law School and lives in the Del Ray part of Alexandria with his wife, Molly.

About the Cover

Old Town Alexandria by Moonlight
By John M. Barber
Fellow, American Society of Marine Artists

This painting shows the *Talisman* departing Alexandria, Virginia, c. 1885, as seen from the foot of King Street. In the scene we see the sailing bark being towed by a steam tug down the Potomac River to begin her voyage to South America for guano, which would be returned to Virginia and used as fertilizer. Steam ferries such as the City of Alexandria shuttled passengers and horse-drawn wagons upstream to Washington and other side-wheel streamers such as *Wakefield* plied the Potomac with passengers and freight. On this evening the waterfront was aglow with gas lamps and busy with activities around the inns, sail lofts, ship chandleries and saloons. *Old Town Alexandria by Moonlight* was published as a limited edition of 950 lithographs in 1994 by the artist.

Over the years the artist has created nearly 1,000 works of original art with 136 of his paintings being published as limited edition prints which are available in art galleries nationwide.

For more information on the artist, please contact:

John M. Barber
10404 Patterson Ave. Suite 205 • Richmond, VA 23238
804-269-3025 • www.johnbarberart.com johnmortonbarber@gmail.com